WHITE LIGHT TAROT ™

The Power Within – Combining Tarot and Reiki

By
Jessica Fisher Willson

With editorial assistance by
Julie House and David Buehler

Brookline, Massachusetts, USA

Library of Congress Catalog Number: 2009929957
ISBN-10: 0-9824839-2-9
ISBN-13: 978-0-9824839-2-3

Published by Sylphar Press, Brookline, MA

Design and Layout by WhiteLightWeb.com

Printed in the United States of America.

Preface

It is sometimes difficult to integrate different systems of symbols. I greatly admire the creative approach of the remarkable White Light Tarot in combining the traditional Major and Minor Arcana, the Chakra system and Reiki teachings. I also find the "keywords" provided at the top of each card to be a helpful addition. Some of the paintings used on the cards are strikingly vivid: <u>The Lovers</u> and <u>The Tower</u>, for example. Others have a more subdued mood, but one which can help the user personally identify with the card. The Fool and The Magician are examples of this. I am sure that this new interpretation of the Tarot will bring light and blessings to many. In addition to the excellent cards, I have found the website http://whitelightTarot.com to have many valuable aids to using this important new deck.

John Granrose PhD
April 26, 2007, Athens, GA.

Dr. Granrose is the past Director of Studies for the C.G. Jung Institute in Zürich, Switzerland, and Emeritus Professor of Philosophy at the University of Georgia. He lectures worldwide on magic, archetypes and Jung's teachings.

Acknowledgements

Thanks must first go to my husband Harvey, without whose steadfast encouragement I would never have ventured so far.

Overall, I am very fortunate that I had the chance to create White Light Tarot, and I am grateful for family and friends who were accepting and supportive even through their secret skepticism.

Specific thanks go to those certain people who had more than their fair share of putting up with my foibles through this lengthy process. To Karine and Cat, my spiritual sisters, thank you for your early insights and trusting in my fortitude. To my friends in the Reiki exchange who supported me through times of doubt, and to my poets Nola and Lo for their open encouragement. To my mother and father, and John who all took time to critique and offer considerable feedback. To my dedicated editors Julie House and David Buehler without whose guidance I would have been utterly lost. To my siblings Sarah and Joey who encouraged me to do what I had to do. Thanks to Chris for his pre-press knowledge, to Chase for his mature understanding, and to Melissa and Michelle for their heartfelt encouragement. To Rhys and Davis for food and outings when I least expected it. And, last but not least, thanks to those early adopters who gave me the courage to keep on writing.

This is not an academic paper, but I've done my best to document and note my research for those who would take it to the next step. When I lack clarity or if I've neglected to refer to a source accurately, please accept my apologies. This document is original research and based upon personal experience.

Jessica Fisher Willson
Full Moon in Sagittarius
Summer Solstice, 2008

iii

CONTENTS

INTRODUCTION

At the center of your being, you have the answer; you know who you are, and you know what you want.
Lao Tzu 6th century BC, Taoist Philosopher

How to Use This Book

In this book, each Tarot card correlates to a chakra. Since chakras are supposed to be energetic representations of our physical state, it seems intuitively fitting that a "random" throw of the cards influenced by our meditative state can show us where we need energetic attention, and what to expect if we use our energy in this way or that.

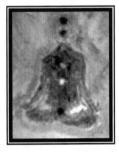

All the same, please note up front that using Tarot and Reiki for healing takes on a few assumptions, and they should never be a substitute for medical attention when medical attention is required.

We Assume When Using Tarot And Reiki:

- That we can help ourselves with "self-talk."
- That we have "higher selves" and "guides" that we can tap into for psychological profiling.
- That psychological problems manifest into physiological problems, and Reiki can help rebalance and ease blocks back into healthy alignment.

9

- That we know the answers to most of our philosophical *"what should I do"* questions intrinsically, but we need validation which can occur by interacting with the Tarot symbols.
- That "random" isn't really "random." A card throw is a message either from our "higher selves" or from our "guides" that we need to recognize.

The bulk of the book is devoted to examining the individual cards starting with the major arcana followed by the four minor arcana suits (Swords, Wands, Cups and Disks) on a card-by-card basis. The associated chakra is noted for each card, and in-depth information is covered in the chakra section of the book. Other topics include caring for the cards, card spreads, and a bit of history.

Reiki Energy

Reiki is the use and manipulation of *healing* energy. According to the proponents of Reiki, ancient healers and enlightened masters like Jesus and Buddha practiced Reiki, although the technique had no name.

Reiki is a healing method that directs psychic and physical energy through our subtle energy conduits (*nadis*) that we may experience as heat. Reiki is hard to describe. It is a hands-on healing technique, but it can be administered over long distances as well. To become a practitioner, Reiki energy has to be "turned-on" by a process of instilling symbols into the initiate by a master teacher.

The Rediscovery of Reiki Energy

Dr Mikao Usui 1865-1926

Dr. Mikao Usui received the symbols of Reiki at the turn of the 20th century. As the story goes, Usui *Sensei* (master) spent many years of study in America, India, China, and his native Japan trying to understand and replicate the healing powers of Jesus and Buddha.

After years of searching the Upanishads, the Vedas, the Gnostics and other scriptures, Usui found texts that described the movement of energies and symbolic hand postures, but the texts did not disclose how to turn this energy on.

At a crossroads as to how to continue, Usui made the pilgrimage from a Zen temple in Kyoto where he lived to Mt. Kumara. There he sat in contemplation for 21 days, trying to figure out what to do next in his quest. Part of the time he spent meditating under a waterfall, which he claimed opened his crown chakra allowing him to receive the knowledge of Reiki.

After many days of fasting and meditating, Usui said he experienced a phenomenal burst of light entering his body. He described the experience as fireballs being shot at his chest in quick succession, and with each fireball, a new Reiki symbol was placed into his body; he fainted from the force of the energy.

When he awoke, he knew he had his answer and the healing technique he had sought. Neither hungry nor tired after his 21-day fast, he only took water from a well at the foot of the mountain, and there he wrote down the symbols that were burned into his being. Eventually, disciples would take the knowledge worldwide and it would become known as Reiki. [1]

Japanese Text of the Five Precepts

THE FIVE PRECEPTS
(PRINCIPLES)

1. Just for today, do not worry.
2. Just for today, do not anger.
3. Honor your teachers, parents and elders.
4. Earn your living honestly.
5. Show gratitude to every living thing.

The Five Precepts, taught to any new Reiki practitioner,

remind one to stay in the present. The emphasis is on mindfulness, honoring life, and our ancestors. Living by the Five Precepts fosters focusing the mind, and calming the spirit.

In a pop-culture comparison, I think that Reiki is like "the Force." In the film *Star Wars*, Yoda describes the Force to Luke by saying:

"Life creates it, makes it grow. Its energy surrounds us and binds us. Luminous beings are we, not this crude matter. You must feel the Force around you; here, between you, me, the tree, the rock, everywhere, yes."[2]

When describing the fundamental ideas behind Reiki (pronounced *ray-key,*) we often break apart the two Japanese characters that make up the word. *Rei* translates to "light" and *Ki* translates to "life-force." The ideas in *Star Wars* of mind over matter, the power of feeling, and that we're all connected are all concepts that form the foundations of Reiki.

There are other ideas related to Reiki that help form the foundation of spiritual truth. Related reflections in the ancient Hindu scripture of the Upanishads talk about the individual soul and the "over-soul"[3] and their interrelatedness. The Upanishads describe how the universal source of all things is also within each of us, or how the microcosm of the self spiritually reflects the macrocosm of the universe and vice versa. "...[T]he ultimate, formless, inconceivable Brahman is the same as our soul, Atman. We only have to realize it through discrimination."[4]

The Upanishads tell us that one path to realization is through the utterance of "OM" which is the divine cosmic vibration that is underlying everything. These sacred texts were the culmination of the Vedas written in Sanskrit over several centuries, by the *rishis* or Hindu sages and seers.[5] The Upanishads are the essence of all the Vedic teachings, starting as early as eighth century BC, almost 4000 years ago.

Buddhism broke away from Hinduism with the teaching of Gautama Buddha in 5th century BC. Usui Sensei was a Buddhist monk and a practicing Christian, but there are clear connections with the philosophical standing of Reiki and Buddhism. The Buddha's teachings include the "Four Noble Truths" and the "Eightfold Path."[6]

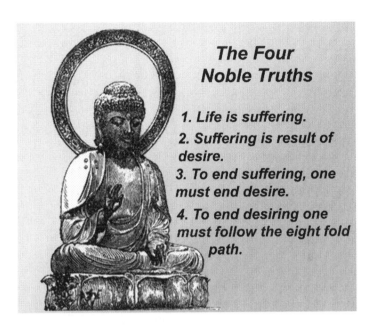

"...[O]ne can stop desiring by following the Noble Eightfold Path: right speech, action, livelihood, effort, awareness, concentration, intention, and views. Consistently following of this path will eventually lead to enlightenment (nirvana)."[7]

Recent discussion includes possible linkage of the early Vedas with Norse and Greek writings as well, spreading as the Indo-European tribes dispersed throughout the continent.

The surrounding cultural context of Reiki is clearly Buddhist, but because Usui was also a Christian, Reiki has bridged the gap philosophically. Reiki abstracts the healing practices from the exacting cultural practices and complex religious philosophies of its Buddhist and Christian antecedents. It thus becomes a single system amiable to any cultural or religious background. The synergy of these ideas creates a view by which we can gain a greater perspective, hence the reason that Reiki chakra energy fits in with a revised Tarot.

Tarot embraces the symbolism of the early Christian church. This is interesting because in the Middle Ages the Roman Catholic Church referred to the Tarot as "the devil's picture book."[8] Tarot, although full of allegorical tales that emphasized ethical behavior, was outlawed partly due to gambling, but more likely because the Tarot referenced pagan customs that the Church was trying to eradicate or envelop into its own form of worship. Nonetheless, having some understanding of the origins of the symbols and their context helps us develop a deeper understanding and broader construct for our feelings when using Reiki-Tarot cards. We can interpret our cultural heritage, our physical, emotional, ethical, and etheric[9] selves as part of the mix.

Tarot's Origins – The Occidental Symbol Set

Tarot's symbolism has its origins in Catholicism, Alchemy, and Greek paganism. Medieval Europe during the Dark Ages (400-800 AD) encountered and succumbed to the spread of Christianity, no doubt to offset disease, poverty, and to reroute and protect stunted trade routes that were no longer viable due to war or economic constriction.

Alchemy Symbols :: Philosopher's Stone Showing its Twin Nature

People who could read and write were rare, the Magi of the age. Trade of Egyptian love spells date back to 500 BC on papyrus, as well as the writings of Pliny the Elder, Galen, Seneca, and other men from antiquity would shape the Church's ethical teachings. Fakes that usurped pagan ritual and current ethical code would also find a place in the libraries of leaders. Paper was a luxury item and esoteric pursuits, like fortune telling by way of magical formulas, became sought after by the rich and powerful.

INTRODUCTION

The Tarot, as it evolved, became a vehicle for interpreting the conglomerate of myths, ethics, and teachings that were common during the Middle Ages. In my view, comparatively, the symbolic structure of the Tarot is very much in keeping with Dante's *Divine Comedy,* written around 1300 in Italian rather than Latin making it much more accessible to the common-man.

The trumps, also called the higher or major arcana, represent the hero's journey, so eloquently spoken of by Joseph Campbell. One starts out a fool or "every man," with the objective of finding final enlightenment in recognizing one's universal "divine light." Dante's Inferno, Purgatory and Paradise, through the first twenty-one trump cards could symbolize the layers of hell (0-7), purgatory (8-13), and heaven (14-21). Put another way, the knowledge of the physical self in the universe gives way to a torturous decision and process of determining what God or heaven means. Allegorical representations of philosophies of the day, like Thomas Aquinas's *Seven Heavenly Virtues* (Faith, Hope, Charity, Fortitude (courage), Justice, Temperance, Prudence) and *Seven Deadly Sins* (Pride, Anger (wrath), Sloth, Greed, Gluttony, Lust, Envy) are literally in the higher arcana. Other literary correlations tied to the Tarot are found in epics such as those of Homer and Ovid. We find imagery that clearly pulls from Greek myth, for example in Cary-Yale Visconti's Tarot which dates from sometime between 1420-1460 and uses Hermes in the trumps.

We know the lineage of Tarot is at least 700 years old, and a popular misconception is that Tarot came from Egypt. However, there is no empirical evidence that definitely connects Egypt to the Tarot, other than that of myth and popular culture in the early 1900's when Egyptology was all the rage. We have examples of Tarot from 13th century Italy and France, and that's about it. As mentioned earlier, one of the older surviving decks is the Cary-Yale Visconti deck. Filippo Maria Visconti commissioned cards in celebration of his soon to be born heir. The child was born – a girl – and when she reached the mature age of twenty, an additional deck was commissioned for her marriage. The decks use family members and the Greek Pantheon to illustrate customs and concepts of good and evil, and the cards were used in a game of chance called Tarocci.

Such was the development of an allegorical deck of pictures that in essence illustrated beliefs and concepts found in the popular culture. The Tarot became a sort of "Bible" for those who could not read. It became a way of divining the future through moralistic tales, and a way of remembering the teachings of the Druids, the Bible, Dante, and Homer as an amalgam of western culture.

The Classical Elements

In the foundations of western culture, we find that the Greeks described the energies that made up the body and the universe. Around 350 BC, Aristotle wrote a treatise where he described the nature of absolutes by looking at causality, potentiality, and actualization in terms of five elements. The five elements each have their natural place in the hierarchy. Aether (divine substance that makes up the heavenly spheres), Fire (hot and dry), Earth (cold and dry), Air (hot and wet) and Water (cold and wet).

Aristotle places the earth at the centre of the uni-universe, followed by water, then air, then fire concentri-concentrically around earth. He describes that when an element is out of its natural place, it will still have natural motion, requiring no external cause, so bodies sink in wa-water, air bubbles rise up through wa-ter, rainwater falls through air, flame

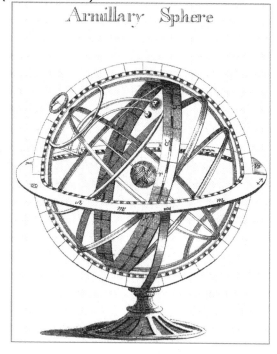
Armillary Sphere

rises in air, and Aether, the heavenly element, has perpetual circular motion.

Similarly, the Upanishads identified these elements respectively as Prithvi, Aappas, Vayu, Thejas and Akash. These elements interacted with appropriate forces to sustain the universe, and collectively were termed "Pancha Bhuthas." The philosophers, by sheer inspiration, tried to unify all these into a coherent picture of space, time and matter. Newton supplied the concept of gravity, which explains all the "natural motions" of Aristotle. Einstein described distance between two events in space-time as $\sqrt{x^2+y^2+z^2+t^2}$, thus unifying space and time. He also gave us $e=Mc^2$ which unites the concept of energy with mass. The quest is not over.

We've Come Full Circle – Scientific Proofs

In our own age of scientific enlightenment, this view of the universe metaphorically describes the same things that scientists like Brian Greene, professor of mathematics and physics at Columbia University and author of *The Elegant Universe* and *The Fabric of the Cosmos*, are grappling with in string theory and the theory of everything. In an interview, Greene described it this way:

"When we say strings are tiny, we generally mean strings that haven't had a huge amount of energy pumped into them. But the more energy you pump into a string, the more widely it will vibrate and, at some point, the longer it will grow. So it's really a question of how much energy the string embodies. Typically they don't embody that much, and therefore typically they are very small."

At the heart of mind-body management is the idea that we have the ability to conceive and conduct ourselves in such a way as to bring about our desired destiny. This is not to say that we don't have "free will," or that outside circumstances don't also influence our lives, but it is interesting to note that there are now scientific proofs of mind over matter. We can put energy into that which we want to grow larger, and we must remind ourselves constantly of this. One way to increase the mind's flexibility and stay open to possibility is by using Tarot and Reiki together as one modality that interlocks healing and intuitive expression.

17

The Psychology of Tarot

Furthering the concepts discussed in the Tarot's Origins section, we can choose to examine a person's psychological profile through the Tarot. The broad strokes of hero's journey are found in the high arcana. These first twenty-one cards divide into three sections, each with seven cards. The beginning is comprised of the "innocent venturing forward" (trumps 1-7), the hero's "inward journey" (trumps 8-14), and finally the hero's reemergence in a "path of community and awakening" (trumps 15-21). The cycle begins anew with the hero helping others on the path.

According to E.B. Weisstub, "Jung's concept of the self is related to the Hindu metaphysical concepts of Atman and Brahman, whose source was the older Aryan nature-oriented, pagan religion."[10]

We can correlate the twenty-one major arcana to the seven major chakras; it seemed only natural to assign each high arcana card with a chakra characteristic, that which is encountered on the journey to self-realization in each of the stages of self-development. If we value the Tarot's interpretation of a situation and its teachings, the major arcana as a psychological tool offers us a way to connect into ourselves. Whatever we may call it, be it our higher selves, our gods, or our ideals, the Tarot as a psychological prop allows us breathing room to comfortably explore any issue in a playful yet sacred way. The Tarot reminds us of ways of being and behaving which bring about our own greater awareness.

The matching of chakra energy to each card along with a keyword to meditate on gives us a clear and concrete path to pursue the development of our subtle energies. In Indian medicine, the three *nadis* (Sanskrit for channel or vein), pingala (right side of the spinal cord, active, male energy), ida (left side of the spinal cord, receptive, female energy), and sushumna (center of the spinal cord, the build up of prana) join to create the subtle body. It is through the nadis that the subtle bodies connect in sheaths that create the aura. The physical body holds the cord (spinal column) in which these energies circulate.

In the east, the body was considered a sacred temple, so surgery was never considered an option. Ways of healing that did not break apart the sacred temple were found, hence the development of energy healing. In the process of manipulating internal energies, physical postures were discovered that maneuver the subtle bodies and the physical body. Mudras are yogic hand postures that assist us in connecting the 72,000 nadis (condiuits) in our hands to our brains. By using these hand gestures, we can manipulate the energy that circulates in our subtle bodies. As mentioned earlier, the three primary conduits described in Indian sacred texts are the ida, pingla, and shusuma nadis which combine to create the Kundalini. The corresponding thinking in Chinese medicine found a series of conduits traced as meridians, and they form the basis for acupressure and acupuncture.

In developing a basis for strengthening our physical self through energy manipulation, we can see that if we join the nadis energy points, that is chakras, to the story of the Tarot, it becomes a pictographic system to restore the body and mind to wholeness through the concentration of energetic bodies.

Tarot Meaning & Symbols - Archetypes

For each of the cards an interpretation honors the old but also makes way for new psychological areas to explore. Psychologist Carl Jung was a pioneer in bringing the ideas of archetypes and collective unconscious to the fore. Interestingly, Philo of Alexandria (20 BC.-50 AD), was the first thinker to employ the term "archetype" meaning more or less that any idea is from God and an imitation of God. Through the etymology of the word we can briefly say that *arche* basically means "origin," or "cause," and that *type* can be traced either to meaning "the position of a leader" or "a casting mould." The Greek form of the word is "archetypos," and the Latin form, "archetypus." Nonetheless, our understanding of the term these days is used in the 19th century Jungian sense as a way of describing ideas that need an empirical approach to cataloging. [11]

In 1917, Jung wrote of "dominants of the collective unconscious." He characterized the collective unconscious as nodal points of psychic energy, and he began using 'archetype' around 1919. A concept that would grow in character to encapsulate his earlier terminology 'primordial image' and

19

'dominant' which he had used in describing mythical, legendary, and fanciful motifs found in fairytales and allegorical
fiction:
"It is this factor which I call the archetype or primordial image. The primordial image might suitably be described as the
instinct's perception of itself, or as the self-portrait of the instinct.
...The primordial image, elsewhere also termed archetype, is
always collective, that is it is at least common to entire peoples or epochs."

Eventually the concept of an "archetype" and the "collective unconscious" would grow beyond fixed symbols of
primordial images to include dynamic processes and univer-
sally recurring patterns of behavior in the psyche:
"Archetypes may be considered the fundamental elements of
the conscious mind, hidden in the depths of the psyche....They are systems of readiness for action, and at the
same time images and emotions. They are inherited with the
brain structure - indeed they are its psychic aspect.
...[The archetype]... as well as being an image in its own
right... is at the same time a dynamism which makes itself
felt in the numinosity and fascinating power of the archetypal
image."[12]
Jung's ideas remain tools to help us explore our own
deeper motivations and yearnings. Dream analysis, collective
symbolism (archetypes), and seemingly random events not
being random (synchronicity) are all tools for processing in-
herent causality.
Jung's concept of "synchronicity" or "meaningful coinci-
dences" was presented in the 1952 paper "Synchronicity —
An Acausal Connecting Principle." We've all experienced it,
where things seem to magically appear or happen when we
need them most. This harkens back to the absolute fact that
we are energy, and we attract what we need into our lives
effortlessly with our minds, either subconsciously or consciously. Just by thinking, we attract or dismiss possibilities
of action by our attitudes, our internal dialog, and our memories; all this influences how we are in the world now, and
what will happen next in our lives. Our ability to sense a
wider array of reality than that which we can verify physically

is part of the justification for using the Tarot as a tool to reach the higher self.

How and Why Tarot Works

When we use the Tarot, we are asking ourselves for answers. At a subatomic level, we're nothing more than concentrated energy and information. We are held together by the ideas of "who I am" and "what we are." If we can accept that we are fundamentally energy and space, then we can accept that we can influence our surroundings.

Let's imagine ourselves as light, a human shaped golden aura and the cards as light too, each with a separate frequency or color. If we visualize everything at the subatomic level, built of energy (light) and space, all intermingling, we can see that when we shift energy onto the Tarot by shuffling the cards, which in and of itself is an energy information source, we are choosing the information that we most want to absorb. If we can accept that we are energy, we can then accept that through the Tarot we are connecting with our greater source of higher mind, our source of information will offer us what we want or need.

Using the Tarot as a tool opens us up to new possibilities that we might not have thought of before. When we have a problem, most of us experience some form of circular thinking, otherwise known as worry. We have trouble trusting that we know the answer or can find help when we need it. But the Tarot connects the dots of what we're really, really thinking about something. It's like extra synaptic activity that we didn't plan on. The Tarot is an information energy bundle, just like we are, an energy bundle to which we have assigned various meanings. The meanings of the cards are human based and emotionally-charged, and when using the Tarot, you will select (at a subatomic level, or subconsciously) the exact information that you need. It's that easy. Because it is emotional content and not intellectual, there is nothing to learn, but there is much to absorb.

By using the Tarot we are consciously deciding to invite possibility into our lives. We are making conscious contact with our higher selves. When we make this conscious effort, it overrides the subconscious level of what generally controls our lives and we are then influencing the possible outcomes to our liking.

Using Reiki and Tarot

Because Reiki is an energy modality, it can help us use Tarot as a diagnostic tool. Used together they indicate what ails us, or what we need to pay attention to emotionally. Each Tarot card depicts an archetype, or a fundamental state of being that we all experience. Additionally, each card boils down to a single word that illustrates and possibly evokes an emotional response. Since each of the seven major chakras connect to particular emotional issues that surface in that body area, we can utilize that information in structuring a healing session. By combining the chakra colors, keywords, and Tarot's archetypal concepts, we are empowered to see what areas in our aura are weak or overcompensating, and we can adjust the energy flow with meditation.

Thoughts Speak Louder Than Words

Although it seems like the universe is the first to act, it isn't so. The universe responds to what we want – *we* are the first to act. If we can really take this to heart, we can create or bring about circumstances that facilitate the creation of our goals, hopes, dreams and desires. But it takes constant vigilance. The law of attraction is very simple to apply, but very difficult to maintain in practice. First, we must cultivate the mindset that will help us banish negative thinking. We have to catch ourselves in the act of negative thinking, change the " this always happen to me" attitude, and reinterpret or reframe the statement into "I am learning something essential from this experience," then add to that statement "I am ready to assimilate the lesson and move on." To determine if it's working, you check in with your feelings. If you feel any discomfort, any anger, any residual resentment, any pain, then the universe will persist in giving more of that same lesson because that's what it thinks we want since that's what we're thinking about. But even if you're not able to release the experience, you will be able to identify it; this is empowering in and of itself, and will lead to release. If you want more peace, better health, better relationships, harmony, and prosperity in your life, then you must "breed" it.

INTRODUCTION

Think happy thoughts, and the universe will follow your instructions.

Shuffling

Shuffling is the most conventional way that you imbue the cards with your energy and your concerns. When you randomize the cards and send energy into them, the cards become a way to examine the state of the questioner's chakras. But remember that even if you don't touch the cards, they may offer a pertinent message via your energy. Theoretically you don't have to touch the cards at all. Your intention is enough to send and receive the proper message. That said, the act of shuffling does put one in a more receptive state because of the rhythmic nature of the act.

To a certain extent, it is for the questioner's comfort that the cards are shuffled. All the same, doing so yields a more accurate reading because it slows the questioner down and allows them a chance to focus on one aspect of the situation. The questioner's energy is transmitted to the cards no matter what, provided it is intended. If the questioner doesn't intend to transmit his or her energy to the cards, then the energy is blocked and the reading will be muted even if the cards were handled.

Any card reading will reflect how much we are willing to instill into the cards, even in long distance readings. The cards act as a barometer or a vehicle for getting a message from our guides or our higher selves. It doesn't matter how the questioner shuffles them, it's just a matter of getting her energy on them in whatever way she can, whether it is by actually touching the cards or by simply sending her energy to the cards by thinking about it.

Appropriate Questions

Anything goes really, but questions about the subject and appropriate behavior will yield the most telling answers. Things like "Am I doing the right thing?" or "Am I on the right path?" or "What was there to learn about this past situation?" will help you recognize next steps, and will delve into the archetypal nature of the hero's journey.

When you are asking about an immediate stressful situation, the cards can offer a fresh perspective to help you analyze your true feelings or unlock pent-up feelings about the situation. Things you might not have realized were lurking beneath the surface will float up.

In asking about situations involving more than one person, statements like "the issue is work," or "the issue is my relationship," work better than "Should I break-up with my boyfriend?" or "Will I get a promotion?" or "Does so and so like me?" That is simply because the cards are parables or philosophical in context. The cards offer us stories in each of their images, and the images unleash unconscious connections.

Usually the cards will give you more information to ponder, or confirm what you already thought. Asking about other people can yield confusing results because the cards are reading what *you* desire and or how *you* feel. So asking about someone else's feelings about you doesn't work as well as asking about yourself.

Reading for Yourself and for Others

Always be respectful and sensitive about what you are doing. When you read for yourself, you are acting as the questioner and the interpreter. Some people feel it is difficult to play both roles at the same time, but if you are clear about your intent, and honest with yourself, then there is no reason you can't interpret the cards for yourself.

If you are interpreting the cards for someone else, be clear with them that nothing bad is going to happen and that the cards are indicators of where one might consider placing or not placing his energy. You are acting as a guide and intermediary between him and his higher self. Don't allow your ego to get involved in the interpretation. Ask the questioner for input as you go, and tell him from the start that the interpretation is like a conversation; the cards can mean various things under various circumstances. Give him an overall impression, and then discuss the various ways the individual cards are interacting, and their meanings, as appropriate.

Before a reading for another person, it is customary to clear the cards. You clear the cards by calling in your energies and intending the clearing. That's it – now the cards are clear of any unwanted energies. If you have a quartz crystal, you might want to tap the Tarot three times with the crystal to confirm that they are clear and grounded. When you put them away, visualize a clear sky or bright white light, then visualize it shrinking down into a sphere around the cards that only your hand can penetrate. This will protect them with light energy, and keep them clean and energized.

Creating sacred space for a reading is not hard. Sacred space is anywhere you declare it to be. Of course, there are some places that are more receptive to being sacred, such as temples, churches and holy gathering places, but they are only more sacred because so many people have defined them as such. The earth is sacred, the universe is sacred, so don't worry too much about creating sacred space for readings or for storing your cards. Simply intend it, visualize white light surrounding the area to clear it, and you're golden. How much the area is shared with other people will determine how much energy you need to expend in keeping a space clear and receptive. Props such as cloths, stones, and feathers can help keep energetic boundaries as necessary.

Storage, Clearing and Protection

When you first get the cards, you might want to clear them by placing them in a favorite window for a day. This energizes them with sunlight and moonlight, or yin and yang energies. The cards are a spirit medium in concrete form. When we use the Tarot, we are connecting with the energy of the human archetypal mind, or unconscious, and possibly with other entities, spirits and energies. Therefore, it is suggested that you place the cards with a favorite stone or a crystal of your choice for grounding. This conveys to the spirit of the cards that they are in the earthly realm. No matter what stone you pick, rocks are from the earth, so placing a stone with the cards helps ground them. Any other special objects will also help them tune into your energy and frequency more.

To store them you can wrap them in cloth or put them in a pretty bag, or box, or simply store them in the box they came in. Whatever you do, be respectful. It is best to keep them in a safe, quiet place, where you have easy access to them. But don't worry too much about it either. They'll be fine wherever they are. You can store your cards anywhere, but storing them somewhere where they are quiet and not crowded is appropriate and respectful.

Tarot Card Spreads

Yes/No Spread

You can program the Aces to be *yes* right side up and *no* reversed. Simply separate them from the deck, program them by telling them your intent (that they are *yes* or *no)* for this question, ask your question, shuffle the four cards, and the more right side up cards you get, the more likely the answer will be yes, and vice versa. If you get a tie, two *yes* cards and two *no* cards, then you've got a "maybe" answer. Once you're done, shuffle them back into the deck and say, "Cancel, clear," to end the programming.

1 card: Meditation or the Crux of the Matter Spread

Pull one card to find out what the day holds, or to get insight into the crux of the matter. This reading can help when you feel like you are getting too much information from other readings. It will clarify what you need to concentrate on or meditate on.

3 cards: Past, Present, Future Spread

The way I learned to lay this spread is from right to left, which is the opposite of how I lay a four-card spread or the Celtic Cross. I think the reason for laying the cards this way is to break up any inertia. It throws our energy off balance, and the three card spread acts like an emotional snapshot of this particular moment in time. To start, clear the cards,

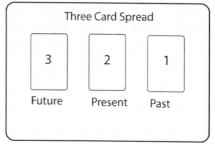

shuffle, cut the deck, and then lay the 1st card to the right. This first card is the past card and it indicates where you are coming from. The 2nd card is the present card. It indicates how you are feeling just now. The 3rd and last card is the future card laid to the left of the other two; it offers the best course of action under the circumstances. This spread is a quick indicator of emotional states or situations and indicates the most likely outcome if you continue on this course of action.

4 cards: What Do I Need to Know Spread

This spread reads like a sentence. It is laid from left to right. It is more of a general life indicator of where you are in the big picture and what you need to concentrate on. The four card spread: 1st card purpose in life; 2nd major relationship; 3rd financial situation; and 4th outcome.

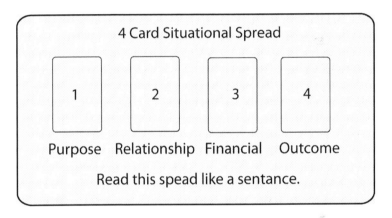

5 cards: Undo the Blockage or the Fifth Element Spread

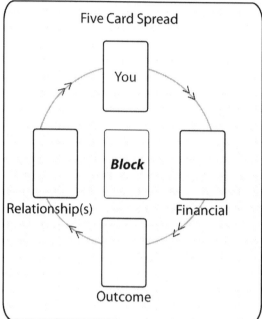

Five Card Spread

You

Block

Relationship(s)

Financial

Outcome

This spread opens the door to any major blockages. The 1st card is where you are or how you're feeling, the 2nd is how your major relationship is impacting the situation, the 3rd is your financial situation, and the 4th is the most likely outcome if you can clear the block which is indicated by the fifth card (called the fifth element or spirit card.) The 5th card is the key or the block that you need to open in order to have the rest of the cards work at their optimum level. To clear the block, concentrate on the chakra indicated and use the keyword as an action word.

7 cards: Chakra Spread

Each card is a message concerning one of the seven major chakras. Each keyword indicates what issues are present in that area. Chakras are sometimes blocked, overactive, or underactive, so if we know where to focus our energy, we can help restore our good health and openness. You can put the keywords and chakra characteristics into a sentence where any energy that is muted is displayed when the card is reversed.

A sample reading:

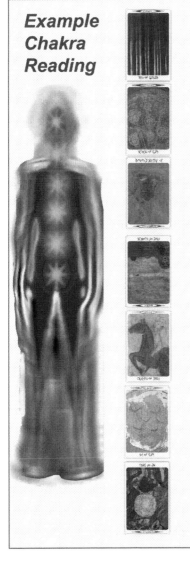

Example Chakra Reading

7. Representing the Crown Chakra [Ten of Wands, keyword finale, chakra root]

6. Representing the Brow Chakra [Seven of Cups, keyword connection, chakra brow]

5. Representing the Throat Chakra [*Reversed:* Awakening, keyword enlightenment, chakra brow]

4. Representing the Heart Chakra [*Reversed:* Five of Swords, keyword shame, chakra root]

3. Representing the Solar Plexus Chakra [Queen of Disks, keyword rescue, chakra solar plexus]

2. Representing Sacral Chakra [Six of Cups, keyword freedom, chakra throat]

1. Representing the Root Chakra [*Reversed*: Ace of Disks, keyword prosperity, chakra heart]

Put the cards in order laying them on top of one another, note which are reversed as that is where something is going on that needs attention energetically. From the cards in the example we can combine the characteristics of the card and the keyword and apply it to the position of the chakra.

There are blocks in tribal connection to *prosperity* (1), you feel that communicating your creativity *freely* (2) is very important, but you use a lot of energy *rescuing* and protecting (3) others. You feel *ashamed* (4) when taking time for yourself and you may not be practicing self love enough. Being able to communicate your *enlightenment* (5) is your goal, but it is difficult if you are too *connected* to other people's goals and visions (6). You need to *finalize* and acknowledge your connections to your root source, love (7).

10 cards: Celtic-Cross Spread

The Celtic Cross is one of the oldest and most well-known Tarot card spreads and is often used for reading a particular situation in order to get a more in-depth reading. First, pick a card to represent the querent or questioner, usually a face card, then shuffle the deck. The next card is laid on top of the question card in the center of the reading. As you lay this card, say, "This card covers you." It represents the initial question. The next card is what is in the balance; it indicates the issue at hand, or the decision that must be made. When laying the card down, say, "This card crosses you." The rest of the surrounding cards are about the questioner's feelings and where they are coming from. Lay the third card above the cross saying, "This card is above you." It indicates the ideal situation the questioner is projecting consciously. Lay the fourth card below the cross saying, "This card is below you." It indicates what is below the surface, what she is doing to influence the situation subconsciously. The fifth card is the past; lay it saying "This card is the past." This may be the root of the problem, or it might be the recent past. The next card, card six, is what is ahead; say, "This card is the future," where she is heading given the current circumstances.

The next four cards indicate how the questioner sees herself, how others see her, what she most hopes or fears, and the best possible outcome. When laying the seventh card say, "This is how you see yourself." This card indicates self esteem, misgivings and confidences. The eighth card indicates how others see her; say, "This card indicates who surrounds you" and it indicates their influences over her. The ninth card shows the questioner's hidden hopes or dreams; when laying this card say, "Your hopes or fears." This card indicates what may hinder or help her efforts. And the final card shows the outcome, what she will take away from this lesson for her efforts or the final yield. When laying this card say, "This card is the best possible outcome."

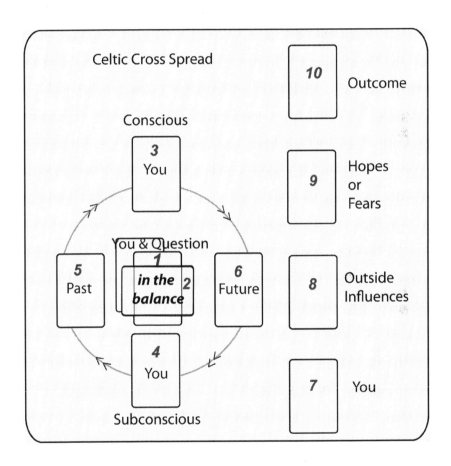

HIGH ARCANA

There are the twenty-two archetypal cards in any given Tarot deck. They are the broad brush strokes that paint everyone's lives. They represent the cosmic laws of karma, and the dogma we use to justify or enforce our behavior. They color the overarching forces that are in effect at the time of the reading. The higher arcana are the 'fate cards,' if you will, or what might be considered outside our immediate influence. They offer clear examples of our best selves and worst selves. Concepts like the seven deadly sins: pride, avarice, extravagance, envy, gluttony, wrath, and sloth can be found here, but the seven holy virtues of courage, generosity, mindfulness, diligence, patience, kindness and selflessness are also found in the twenty-two archetypes of the high arcana.

The Fool

Keyword: Everyman
Chakra: Crown, Violet

The innocent businessman (fool) steps out of the train to seek his fortune in the green forest of possibility. The train platform is the entry into the world of concrete possibility and manifestation. The fool is released from the spirit train and his journey begins anew under his own aspect. Rather than spirit directing or carrying him, he is now ambling under his own power. Behind those green forest trees of possibility are meadows of self-doubt, which the fool can meander by, get caught up in, feel overly exposed by, or brightly run through without a care. What he ends up doing will be determined by his awareness.

The platform sign says "Mind The Gap" but the Fool knows that his destiny can take him anywhere. Zero is likened to the ouroboros. It is the beginning and the end. The innocent must always remember that the first step is a big one, but in order to start any journey one must be willing to believe in himself and take that first step. Will he be foolish and get caught up in the entanglement of thorns that so often lead us astray - seeking money and power? The message of the Fool is to be mindful of the gap between reality and possibility, to not get caught up or bogged down in reality, and to maintain innocence and welcome possibility.

Reversed: You're not remembering who you are; you are acting foolish. When we don't remember who we are, we can act out in ways that disconnect us with spirit. In other words, in some way we are acting foolish. For some reason, you are

34

not happy with the way things are, and you are not willing to trust that things will improve. Instead your tendency is to berate yourself or others for circumstances outside of your control. To fix the situation, the one thing that you must do is reconnect with your divine goodness. To do this, find a way to trust that everything will work out for the highest good of all concerned.

The Magician

I THE MAGICIAN

Keyword: Co-create
Chakra: Brow, Indigo

The Magician manifests and co-creates his reality with love and spirit. Rings of green and violet circle him as he vibrates love and spirit. He channels spirit through the heart chakra and allows it to flow out through his fingers. The image suggests he might be at a computer workstation on a field of green, which represents love and possibility. One is the 'manifest will' in union with the divine. The divine in achieving the power and knowledge to create does so through the Magician.

He conducts the symphony that will transform air into matter. He directs pure energy and drive into achieving a goal. Knowledge is used to good purpose. The creator (magician) uses tools of his time, in this case possibly a computer, to create a new reality and to bring about a change in a physical way.

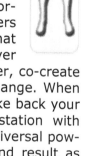

Reversed: You are manifesting your own sorrow. You have far more control over the situation than you give yourself credit for. Don't underestimate the power of gratitude and for-giveness. Bestow them on yourself and others every chance you get, and soon you'll find that things are aligning the way you desire. Never beseech or ask the universe for something; rather, co-create the situation that will bring about the desired change. When you plead, you are not in a position of power. Take back your power by sharing the responsibility of manifestation with other people, your higher self and any greater universal pow-ers that you believe in. You do influence the end result as your attitude is what others respond and react to. Be your own best advocate, take time when you need it, give thanks when you want something, as it is a gift that we can desire, and forgive yourself and others for any shortcomings. In so doing, you realign yourself with spirit or your own true blissful nature. Give it time; things will change for the better.

The High Priestess

Virgin

2 THE PRIESTESS

Keyword: Virgin
Chakra: Sacral, Orange

Representing communication through air and spirit, the High Priestess acts as the conduit through which nature speaks. She is the voice of the bird song, the brook, the wind. She harnesses nature and conducts it through her body. The Egyptian headdress suggests the power of the priestess and her manifestation as the essence of the human deity: holy, ideal, expressive. The High Priestess is the first in the triad of women archetypes of virgin, mother, and crone. Full of exuberance for life she relies on her noted attributes of dexterity, intelligence, and charisma in embracing life. She is a vestal virgin by choice, and keeps her kindling available for matters of spirit alone. She trusts her intuition, and she acknowledges the moon's guidance in ritual which helps her to maintain connection with the natural world, reality and illusion, and her goddess-given psychic abilities.

The High Priestess is associated with the hunt, sexual attraction and energy, the moon, and Aphrodite. When seeking connection with your higher self, call upon the High Priestess to connect you to your inner Aphrodite.

Reversed: You have fallen prey to the illusion that the physical world is all that is real. You perhaps feel disconnected from the world, and so have taken refuge in a reality vs. illusion discussion with yourself. You need to remember that we only experience a percentage of reality as physical. For example, sounds that are made by elephants or dolphins to communicate are not within our auditory range. Does that mean they do not exist because we cannot experience them? No, we have

scientific tests that allow us to visualize them, and so we can prove that there are sounds outside of our range. Just as we can observe the reaction of a dog to a high-pitched whistle, we know that something is there.

The lesson here is not to discount your abilities, both physical and non-physical. For some reason you have given in to the feeling of being disconnected from your higher self. Take comfort in the earth's presence, feel the wind in your hair and remember that there is more to this life than the physical. Trust that you do have psychic abilities and start the reconnection process by taking a walk in nature. Check what phase the moon is in, and think of yourself as being that way too. Meditate on your life mirroring the phasing of the moon. If the moon is full, in some way you're full. If it is a sickle, then perhaps something in your life needs to grow larger, or diminish away. Remember, this is just a phase.

The Empress

Keyword: Mother
Chakra: Root, Red

She sits in front of a candle flame; her golden aura is visible around her crown. She is holy. She sits deep within the cave of gestation in meditation. The inner womb is warm and flows with red blood, pulsing a calming rhythm. Often associated with growth, menstruation, birthing and spring, she is the spirit that is evoked in planting rituals. The seed is sown in the dark earth, during the full seed moon in April or May. In ancient agricultural rituals, the sex act would take place in a frenzied festival during full moon, right before sowing the fields to ensure a good harvest. The Empress is no prude. She is a sexual being who is mother to the world, both bawdy and refined. She shines as the one most capable of fostering your dreams into reality.

Grow with her. The Empress is the second in the triad of women archetypes. Allow her to nurture you, for she is the ultimate mother, nurturer, and caregiver. She is the spirit of our mother earth. Her rivers and oceans are her blood, her growing things are life giving. Follow her and go inward to gestate, create, and nurture your dreams. The female's ability to harbor life in her womb is our species' physical way of expressing manifestation. Regardless of your gender, you have the ability to nurture; in fact it is in your nature to nurture. Nurture yourself and give thanks to the earth. Know that she loves you, she who is the keeper of the sacred flame. She holds dear all of creation including yours, she is fertility without measure. She exemplifies the feminine prowess of communion.

Reversed: Are you feeling unloved? Perhaps you need a little nurturing. Difficult though it may seem, looking to others for comfort won't work. You need to go inward and reconnect with your ability to nurture from within. You perhaps crave connection with a loved one, or desire a relationship with someone out of reach. Whatever it is that is making you feel unloved, you need to distance yourself from that thing and that feeling. Just take a breather. The most reliable person in your life is you. You're the only one who can make you happy, so resolve to reconnect with yourself and nurture the connection. If you are feeling lonely, light a candle and watch the flicker of the flame, feel the warmth that emanates from the soft glow, and breathe in the sweet perfume of a favorite oil rubbed on the outside of the candle. Cinnamon or clove oil on a red candle will help reconnect you with your base chakra. Your tribe will find you soon, and bring you home. Your base chakra needs clearing and your heart has been holding too many sorrows; allow the flow of the wax to clear your mind and heart and know that you are very loved.

The Emperor

Keyword: Father
Chakra: Solar Plexus, Yellow

The archetypal father figure is held in high esteem by his tribe. He enforces the image of character, fortitude, and control. In truth, he is an idealist, and quite loving, but he is seen as quite fierce. He holds a golden object in his hand, perhaps a drink, perhaps a remote control. No matter what the object, it is an expression of his command over his dominion. He wields this power leisurely and effortlessly. He is stern but loving, choosing to instruct rather than censure when challenged. Others must observe the rules he makes, but he endeavors to rule by example, demonstrating the exemplary behavior of a just and humane ruler, and asking no more of you than he would of himself. A falcon is at his shoulder, ready to do his bidding. The falcon is a symbol of protection and vigilance, ever watchful for correct conduct.

If you show loyalty, humility, and fealty to this great ruler, you will receive loyalty, protection, and instruction on how to conduct yourself and perhaps fearlessly lead your tribe. Look to him when you seek to act as an authority, look to him when you seek a promotion or to finish a difficult task. He will help you stay the course and do your best.

Reversed: You may feel that you have disappointed someone whom you look up to, or you may feel you have been judged in some way. Know that the ill feelings will pass, and the action you take now will determine how you are perceived here after. The most important thing is to reestablish your self-esteem when something bad happens. How you feel about yourself will color your world perception. If things have gone awry in some way, figure out the lesson that the event is teaching you. Everything happens for a reason. Sometimes it may seem like a cosmic reason, outside of your control; sometimes it's because of human emotions. The Emperor, like all good fathers, wants the best for you and he expects you to learn from your mistakes. How you handle life is up to you, but if you face it head-on, as best you can, with determination and love, you'll find the resilience you need to lead your life on the path of virtue. This is what the Emperor expects of you. So forgive yourself of any shortcomings, and resolve to do better. Accept the challenge life offers with the Emperor to help you find your way.

The Hierophant

5 THE HIEROPHANT

Keyword: Knowledge
Chakra: Throat, Light-Blue

Hieros="holy"; phant="one who shows."

The law according to universal truth is not man's law. The Hierophant is the evaluator and keeper of these truths for mankind, and the keeper of sacred knowledge. Trust that you are learning from the wellspring of the source. He knows all religions, and he engenders harmony amongst them in an effort to seek the higher truth. That said, the Hierophant represents the institutionalization of universal law. Everything that is good about organized religion, community support, feelings of belonging, and the belief in good works or helping others is part of what the Hierophant represents. But he is more than that, for he interprets that law and thereby becomes the keeper of our humanity. He organizes and sanctifies society's beliefs as a whole. He represents those who will ultimately become the oppressors before they oppress.

When belief systems are codified they become limiting and stagnate. Babylon was the first civilization to codify its laws, calling it the Code of Hammurabi (ca. 1760 BC). Other examples of codification include the Torah, Hindu Law, Quran, Bible, and in China the Tang code. The point is that these systems do need to be developed and codified or cemented in stone, but like stone they can break. The Hierophant knows this, and he knows that we must follow the spirit of the law and not the letter of the law. Universal truth doesn't change, but it is flexible and has more than one meaning. Interpretation changes, and better ways of expressing universal truth is what the Hierophant

shows us is holy. Keep fluid and seek to live by the spirit of the law, not the letter of the law.

Reversed: Organized religion and government create an environment where oppression of the minority in favor of the majority is too often found. Interpretation that fails to nurture growth is dangerous for the society as a whole. When you get this card, know that the Hierophant sees that you are being oppressed. There may not be any way to rectify the situation easily and it may take time for others to see your point of view. His council is to steady-on and know that if what you believe is the right course, people will come around and agree with you eventually. Things will change, so clear away what misconceptions you can, and look for small ways to forge a new path.

The Lovers

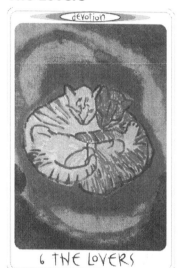

devotion

6 THE LOVERS

Keyword: Devotion
Chakra: Heart, Green

The Lovers card is also known as the card of the brothers. The image of the cats curled up in a circle is indicative of the ying-yang symbol: the uniting of yin and yang, wholeness, experience of higher self through union, the passionate joining of heaven and earth. Harmony, balance, and passion are the principles that drive this card. An unconventional image for lovers or brothers for some, but one that echoes the circle, the balance, the ease, and essential love (compassion as well as passion) that is conceptually associated with the lovers. When you get this card, you have a decision to make. The reasoning here is that there is a choice when one gives herself over to passion, be it romantic love or a political cause. But if we look at the card in the context of the brothers, with the interpretation that there is a decision to be made, we see that the decision could involve cooperation and compassion.

Depending on the question and the position of the card, the interpretation will vary, except that it will always involve more than one person, and a choice that will influence both parties. The decision must not be made lightly. The situation has come full circle in some measure. The ideal is to stay in harmony with the other person and create a union that is stronger than either of you alone. Consider how you can best strengthen and harmonize your life. If this involves someone else, express your position compassionately, and if they are truly your friend, they will respond in kind.

Reversed: When the Lovers card is reversed it doesn't necessarily mean that the love affair is over. The general interpretation is disharmony: something is amiss, something isn't being said, or perhaps something is being misinterpreted. There is a stifling, choking feeling with this card, like a weight on your chest. Release is called for; whether it is in a conversation in the board room or in the bedroom doesn't matter. There is an insidious energy that is discouraging harmony and needs to be eradicated. Take the first step in identifying what you bring to the mix. If you are the victim and not being understood, then make a point of being under-stood. If you must, be brave and walk away from an unhealthy situation. Whatever is going on, disharmony is indicated. Concentrate on healing yourself. A small positive action that will enable healing and shielding your heart can be accomplished with something green. A stone necklace made of Amazonian, Emerald, or Aquamarine could help activate the heart area, as could a necklace made of Rose Quartz. A green 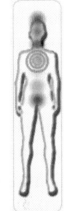 shirt, tie or scarf can also help. The green or pink item should be worn near the chest to activate the heart chakra. Green tea and walks in green areas will also help heal the spirit and clear the system of toxicity.

The Chariot

Striving

7 THE CHARIot

Keyword: Striving
Chakra: Solar Plexus, Yellow

The Chariot today is a fast car, and as a symbol it conveys a strong sense of speed, daring, skill and power. Your journey is underway, your goals are set and you are in control of your vehicle. "Stay on target," as the star fighter says in *Star Wars*, and keep focused on achieving your goals without being reckless. Reckless goal-oriented behavior is rampant in our go-getter society. In our culture we are so goal-oriented that we forget to participate in the journey. It sounds funny to say, but if you focus on the journey, then the quest will take care of itself. We all have things that we have to do, somewhere to be, and something that was due yesterday. Goals are great, but don't let them get in the way of enjoying the process of getting there. Don't let your goals take priority at the expense of your health. If you concentrate on driving and taking care of your car rather than on the destination, you're likely to be more alert, less harried and more in control when you arrive at your destination. So think of the Chariot as telling you not to fear, you're almost there. Now, check the oil and "fill-'er-up," but don't forget to take in a little of the scenery along the way.

Reversed: When you have a wreck, you feel broken and shaken to the core. Fear, arrogance, and reckless behavior are common bedfellows. If you get the Chariot reversed, you have either skidded to a halt in some manner or you're about to crash. This card is giving you explicit instructions to slow down in some area of your life. Get over to the slow lane for a while. Slow down or you'll wind up in the break down lane.

Justice

Keyword: Fearless
Chakra: Throat, Light-Blue

The image of Martin Luther King Jr. is used for the Justice card because he has come to symbolize a just and forthright nature. What is striking is when we experience cosmic justice the content of our character is being tested. Our character is what we are here to develop. It is what we really own. We are asked to build it in this life, and it is our task to live up to the dream that Dr. King so eloquently discusses. This card often appears when our ethics are being tested. Justice affirms that you have the means and the character to fund a will and a way to do what is right, especially when there seems there is no easy way to do the right thing. Although universal justice doesn't always run in accordance with human justice, there is always an equitable balance achieved. The laws of karma also apply to this card; depending on the context when you get this card, it could be signaling the beginning or completion of a cosmic cycle.

Justice is one of the four cardinal virtues (justice, prudence, temperance, and fortitude/strength). Plato, Saint Ambrose, Saint Augustine and Thomas Aquinas all wrote on the nature of a moral life. The word *cardinal* comes from the Latin *cardo,* which means *to hinge*, so cardinal truths were behaviors that our moral life hinged upon. Justice is such because it is humanly achievable through effort aided by grace. With grace on our side, we are capable of great compassion and achievements, all the sweeter if they help others to realize their aspirations as well. When we speak out against oppression, poverty, greed and discrimination we are helping to create a just world. When we intercede, all the more so. When you get this card, know that you are experiencing justice in it's highest form. If you are called upon to act, then do so with integrity. Justice can be painful however, and it isn't an easy road. If you choose this course you will be supported by grace, but it may not feel like it. Just remember your resolve is being tested, and you add to the greater good of humanity when you seek justice and act honorably.

Reversed: You may feel you've been treated unjustly or unfairly, or perhaps you didn't give someone the benefit of the doubt. Some kind of bias, discrimination, or, at its worst, corruption is happening. Justice upside down is a clear indication of the world out of balance. This can be in mental or emotional attitude, feeling the general unfairness of life, physical health (as in "I work out, why can't I lose weight?") or financial health, but something is out of whack and needs attention. Whatever it is that needs your attention, take it head-on and act fairly to yourself and others. As you change your attitude to the most impartial stance you can take, the anger and hurt will begin to melt away because you are doing your best. Stay in control and walk away from situations where you feel put upon. Fight for those who need your help, but always remember that you need to give to yourself too, otherwise you'll burn out and have nothing left to offer. It is not always kindness that people most desire, but rather to be treated fairly and with respect. Endeavor to do so, and the world will reflect back in kind.

The Hermit

Keyword: Seeker
Chakra: Heart, Green

The Hermit is the androgynous keeper of self-knowledge. In the Hierophant, knowledge faces outwards; for the Hermit it faces inwards. In the feminine guise, the Hermit completes the three faces of the goddess. The High Priestess is the maiden, the Empress is the matronly mother figure, and the Hermit is the Crone, Grandmother, or Wise Woman. The Hermit has completed most of life's tasks, and does not seek anyone's approval or thanks. The Hermit is a guide, and therefore does not need to seek solitude for himself, but neither does the Hermit fear being alone. Having moved beyond the ascetic virtues of the Hanged Man, the Hermit can interact with the world, but as his title implies, he has chosen exile in order to deepen his connection to intuition. He uses insight to lead us through our own terrors and into the light of inner wisdom. Complete as a bodhisattva, the Hermit gives back to the world by being the keeper of the light at the end of the tunnel. With the beehive on his back, he is also the keeper of the bees of immortality and creativity as they are the "birds of the muses."

He leads us to ourselves through intuition. When you get this card, you probably need some alone time. Time for circumspection is hard to come by, but the Hermit suggests you need to go inward and honor what you already know is true. You may have had a flash of inspiration, and now know something more about who you are or the situation you're in. Taking time alone to think about things allows us time to gain perspective. When we act with a clear understanding of ourselves and a situation, we act wisely rather than rashly. Listen to the hum of the bees on the Hermit's back, they intone *OM*, the universal sound of peace. The sweet honey of

51

self-knowledge is yours. Just get quiet within yourself, and don't be afraid; the Hermit is there to guide you.

Reversed: Feeling disassociated, having social anxiety in groups, experiencing depression, or listening too much to your inner critic are at issue when the Hermit 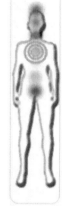 appears reversed. The Hermit reversed can also indicate a problem facing up to your own expectations, or problems in communication or commitment to others. If you get the Hermit reversed, you need to test whether you're acting hastily and hostile towards others at work or at home. Your expectations aren't in line with what is going on in life. You need to adjust your point of view. Sometimes this card indicates you're feeling lonely, and if that's the case, don't despair. Take someone out for coffee, or go to an upscale shop and talk about your color palette, or go to a lecture at the library. Find a small way to reconnect with people, but do it slowly, and listen to the inner voice that loves and appreciates you, not the inner critic. Silence that mean old inner critic if it's too loud by intoning "OM" until you are at ease in your own body and the universe. Sigh and repeat.

The Wheel of Fortune

Keyword: Cycles
Chakra: Heart, Green

Evidence of the wheel dates back to 8000 BC in Asia; the oldest artifact is from Mesopotamia from 3500 BC, and in India, spinning wheels were used as early as 1000 BC. Mahatma Gandhi used a small tabletop spinning wheel to demonstrate self sufficiency, and it became a symbol of the Indian Independence Movement. Interestingly, this style of spinning wheel is called a 'Charkha,' and comes from the same root as the word 'chakra' which also means "spinning wheel."

The wheel also functioned as a metaphor for the cosmos (mandala) in many cultures, and Jung used mandalas as a way of getting in touch with the unconscious self. He believed the act of painting mandalas had therapeutic applications for discovering underlying patterns in behavior. The concept of cycles, or patterns, probably came from observing the moon and its cycles. Early calendars and timepieces were on wheels. Reincarnation, fortune, fate, and eternity are all tied to the object metaphorically. Another well-known symbol in India is the Ashoka chakra which has twenty-four spokes (like the hours in a day.) It is known as the dharma chakra, and each of the spokes represents one of the twenty-four virtues: love, courage, patience, peacefulness, kindness, goodness, faithfulness, gentleness, self-control, selflessness, self sacrifice, truthfulness, righteousness, justice, mercy, graciousness, humility, empathy, sympathy, godly knowledge, godly wisdom, godly morality, reverential fear of God, and faith that God is good.

The core idea is that of the cycle and the continuous dynamic nature of life. The Blood, Sweat and Tears lyric "What goes up, must come down. Spinning wheel, got to go round," illustrates the essential message of this card, as does Ecclesiastes 3:1 "...a time for every purpose under heaven." Like a revolving door, we only see a small section of the whole. When you get this card, a cycle is coming to a close and a new one is beginning. Concentrate on correcting any sluggish spinning in your chakras. We are only here for a short time in this particular guise so remember that this moment is just a phase. The life cycle: birth, life, death and rebirth continuously repeat until full awareness is realized and we understand the true nature of reality.

Reversed: When you get the Wheel of Fortune upside down, it doesn't mean you are marked as unfortunate forever, but it does mean there is a counterproductive element or slow down in your life. You may feel a bit stagnated, turned around or topsy-turvy about an important relationship. The Wheel doesn't run counter clockwise often; when it does, it's like the tick of a second hand on an old-fashioned watch, a hesitation, a tick back and then a tick forward again, slowly marking the passage of time. Sometimes we have to take one step back to start moving forward again. If there has been an event where you acted counter to your inner nature, "ate your words," or "bit your tongue," you may feel ill-fated, but this will pass. To speed up the unfortunate set-back, you need to counteract the cycle. Reverse engineering is when you take apart the object to discover how it's put together. This is something that we sometimes need to do with our emotional life. To do this you can look at your reaction in a given situation. Write it down like a story, then substitute other people for the key players in the story. Examine how the story changes when you change the people involved. You may be able to quickly discover what went off course and get the wheels of fortune back on the right track.

Strength

Keyword: Manifestation
Chakra: Root, Red

As a young lawyer and student of Hindu philosophy, Gandhi was all too aware of the social injustice that the British imposed upon the disparate groups of people in India. Over the course of years, he would develop and write about his beliefs in Satyagraha (non-violent resistance). Gandhi becomes such an example of these techniques that it led to his becoming the father of the Indian Independence Movement which eventually unified the nation through peaceful civil disobedience and ended the tyranny of British rule in India.

Strength is not always about physical prowess, more often than not it is about character. Being a person of character means making ethical decisions that increase the common good. Making the right choice is sometimes difficult, and sticking to it can be even harder.

Saying no to a child whom you love, leaving a relationship that you know isn't working, sticking to a diet, quitting smoking...all of these things take great character. But facing up to our fears of being rejected, being on our own, or without the neural transmitter pleasure crutch that we are accustomed to is what we must do in order to grow and continue to stay strong. This card portends a change is necessary and it will take great strength to see it through. When Strength comes up in a reading, there is probably an ethical decision before us. We manifest our destiny through our decisions, and our decisions emanate from the core essence of our being. Most decisions are made out of habit; if we've had success in some area we tend to do that again.

Our brain's neural pathways are set up in this way, and decision-making is often based on a chemical response. Plain and simple, pleasure or pain outweighs our actual thoughts. What this means is that it takes constant vigilance and focus to make a decision about something when you don't know what the outcome will be, or when it isn't pleasurable. That's where visualization comes in. When you're trying to accomplish something difficult or new, a very helpful technique is to visualize a successful outcome. This physiologically sets up the neural pathways and allows us to develop an experience where none existed before, as it increases the pleasure response in that area, giving us a neurological "fighting chance." Since our decisions are based on our experiences, you might need to create the experience before you can accomplish the task. For example, if you want to lose weight, visualize yourself saying no to cake while wearing your skinny jeans. That creates the experience. Have conviction in your decisions and you will grow in strength of character and experience to keep yourself fortified. Gandhi changed a nation; we can all change our minds, our hearts, and our lives if we'll only put our brains to the task.

Reversed: This card reversed would seem to indicate weakness, but actually it isn't that simple. When you get Strength reversed, it can mean you're experiencing a lack of resolve or a feeling of inadequacy. The problem is that you need to reassess the situation and make a new decision based on your assessment. If you strangle yourself by not allowing wiggle room and by only seeing things as black or white, good or bad, then you're missing all the colors of the rainbow. There are many paths to the same outcome; allow yourself the room to expand your responses. Sometimes we have to be cruel to be kind, but other times we really need to give into kindness. Reassess the situation, and don't blame yourself or others for what has already happened, but move on and act with courage.

Sacrifice

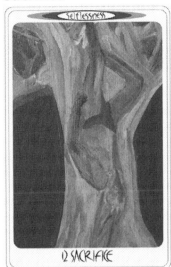

Keyword: Selflessness
Chakra: Brow, Indigo

In order to know the infinite mind which lies beyond the personality, one must sacrifice or surrender the ego self to the higher self. In many mythologies, there is a quest for knowledge beyond birth, life and death. This information is brought back from the divide via a tribe's appointed shaman. Jesus hung on the cross, and Odin hung on the tree of knowledge. Both defied death and brought back sacred knowledge. Another story about the hanging of deities is recorded by Pausanias, and tells of the legendary beginnings of the Kaphyae ritual of "hanging Artemis." Children at play hung her image in the cypress trees sacred to the goddess, possibly for their regenerative powers, as swamp cypress look like a forest fire has decimated them during the winter months. The children were perhaps calling upon the goddess to restore the trees. In any case, the men finding the children with an image of the deity hung upside down in the forest became worried that this was sacrilegious behavior, so they stoned the children to death. Artemis in turn, angered by the men's harsh reaction, cursed the women with infertility, and the oracle at Kaphyae told them that in order to restore fertility, the goddess required that they make it a custom to hang her image in the trees to atone for death of the innocents.

So we have stories of resurrection, trees with regenerative powers, and the sacrifice of the innocent. But there is even more to the story. In addition to the shaman's position in society as magician or god, there is the physical position of the body to consider too.

The theme of sacrifice by hanging is ancient, as is the form of the *fylfot*, which looks like a swastika but with shorter legs. This ideogram is one of the oldest markings found in

Greece, more than 3000 years old, and it is similar to the symbol used by Native American Anasazi to represent the sun. Etymologically, 'fylfot' is Old English and is related to the Norse word meaning "many footed." The reason to mention the fylfot here is that the Hanged Man's legs take on the form of the fylfot. The form is also known as Brigit's cross for the Celtic goddess who is another form of Freya. "The ... spectrum of meaning is centered around *power, energy, and migration*. It is closely associated with the triskellion ⚡ and ↻, thus with tribal migrations."[13]

Besides the story of Jesus, which is well-known in Western culture, there are many other stories of resurrection and knowledge. Let's look at the Norse myth of Odin. Odin hung on the world tree Yggdrasil (which means "Ygg's horse"). The horse is a symbol for the gallows, as in the horsemen of the Apocalypse, but the horse is also a symbol of "fleet footedness" or being fast, strong and honorable. In this instance the fylot (the crossed leg) is a metaphor for Odin's horse Sleipnir who had eight legs, and was the fastest horse in the universe.

In the myth, the hidden knowledge Odin acquires is that of the Runes. The word 'rune' literally means "secret wisdom." Already being the god of war, Odin knew that the only thing that could defeat him was knowledge. Therefore, he sacrificed himself to acquire that which could defeat him, becoming the god of wisdom and knowledge as well. For nine days and nights he hung on the world tree with self-inflicted wounds, taking no food or water until he saw the reflection of the runes in the waters of life that run beneath the world tree.

From *The Norse Eddas, the Saga of the Gods:*

"Wounded I hung on a wind-swept gallows
For nine long nights,
Pierced by a spear, pledged to Odhinn,
Offered, myself to myself
The wisest know not from whence spring
The roots of that ancient rood.
They gave me no bread,
They gave me no mead,
I looked down;

with a loud cry
I took up runes;
from that tree I fell. "

So the combined meaning of the symbols is that of a sacrificial death in order to quickly gain god's knowledge. Each of us throughout our lives plays out the notion of a fleet sacrificial death and resurrection; we migrate to our new lives by renewing our connection to our higher selves. In order to regain our personal power and energy we must experience the migration of the soul. When you get this card you are playing the innocent in some aspect of your life. As an innocent, you disregard the influence you have over your own life. You blame others for misfortunes that befall you and disregard the responsibility you must take on to live wisely. The innocent must be sacrificed in order to acknowledge you are the co-creator of your own life.

The true sacrifice is to let go of ego and personality in favor of finding a deeper understanding of yourself. Value your sacredness by finding that spark of the bodhisattva in yourself. To heed the call of this card is the formidable task of "letting go and letting god." Or put another way, becoming comfortable in the "wisdom of insecurity" as Alan Watts called it.

Reversed: You may be holding on to life too hard, and trying to make things happen when it isn't yet time. You need to let go of desired outcomes and allow the flow of psychic energy to catch up with you. Trying to make things happen is fine, but it needs to be in the context of co-creation. When things aren't working out well, you need to let it go or the universe will give you more of the same. Relinquishing control doesn't mean giving up on your goals, it means allowing others to help you find the right answers, and allowing the form of how you get there to migrate. Sometimes we feel like our way is the only way to do something, so we have trouble accepting other approaches. When we get in this state of mind, we are disconnected from flow and our own innate ability to attract the psychic forces that we need to reach our goal. When you get Sacrifice Reversed it means that you're not willing to let go and let it flow.

Death

Keyword: Rebirth
Chakra: Crown, Violet

Death is the ending of a cycle. In the context of a Tarot reading it does not portend someone's actual death. What it indicates is the diminishing of energy in an area of one's life. It indicates the need to move on or to let go of some aspect of life that isn't working any longer. Forgiveness goes hand in hand with death, just as reawakening to a new spiritual dawn does once the passing has taken place. When we let go of a cherished desire we often need to mourn its passing, just like the passing of a loved one.

The angel of death is there to comfort us and lead us back into the darkness of gestation, so that we can be reborn into the light. It takes time to be reborn, so learning patience is part of the process. In the White Light Tarot's image of death, the character is a woman.

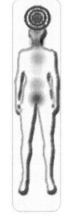

She is painted blue because in many traditions the color blue is associated with release. She has breasts to remind us that she is nurturing and that she is really there to bring about our rebirth. She holds a dream catcher that allows her to catch those dreams that can still be realized while those that are no longer valid slip through. The dream catcher doubles as the wheel of fortune reminding us of the cycles of life, and that where there is death, there is regeneration. A cycle of rebirth is always at work in our lives. She wears the ouroboros snake of regeneration around her neck which reminds us of our immortality. Snakes remind us that we must shed our dead skins every now and again to become renewed. She is the death head, but she holds the nourishment for the next generation in her breast. Without death there would never be regeneration, reincarnation, recycling, evolution, or a single revolution of the wheel.

In the Muslim tradition, Azrael (the angel of death) is also portrayed as the cleverest of the archangels. Similar in nature to Loki in the Norse pantheon or Coyote in the Navajo, Azrael is a trickster. One story in the Qur'an demonstrates this aspect of Azrael's nature. God asked the four archangels Michael, Gabriel, Uriel, and Azrael to gather seven handfuls of dirt from the base of the Tree of Life in the Garden of Eden. Three of them would gather two handfuls of earth, while the last would only bring one handful. Michael and Uriel immediately began to argue over which of them would carry two handfuls. Gabriel tried to step in as a mediator, so Azrael snuck away and gathered all seven handfuls of dirt by himself, putting them in a bag and taking them to God alone. This demonstrates that Death can be a trickster, but if you allow Death's help in your life you will speed your reconstitution and regain your power all the quicker, and in heaping handfuls.

The Death card is the thirteenth card in the Tarot. The number thirteen has associations with the number of moons in an annual cycle in 28-day increments. The idea of transformation is once again indicated as the moon is a reminder of the cycles of transformation. When you get the Death card, examine what areas of your life need to cycle away, and what areas need regeneration and transformation. Trust the angel of death to care for you and respectfully bury that which needs to be reseeded. She will help you let go of your burdens, release them to her and know that this process is just the diminishing of the light now so that you can be, grow, change and blossom anew.

Reversed: Let go of whatever it is you're holding onto that isn't working in your life. Something is holding you back, and it is leading you into stagnation and draining your energy. When you get Death reversed it indicates a lack of trust and pitting your will against everyone else's. The universe is asking that you let go of the pain, the hassle and the need to control the situation. When you let go, you allow new growth to blossom. When you no longer need to control something, it can transform in miraculous ways that you cannot foresee. Trust that if you 'let go and let god' something good will come out of it in some manner. The hard part is allowing whatever it is to unfold without your intervention. If you must let go of a relationship, a job, a child, a cherished desire, know that a better circumstance will arise when you are ready. You must allow the passage, and part of that is mourning the loss. There is a lesson in letting go and trusting that our best and finest natures will surface when we trust our higher selves or 'god' to help us co-create the world. There are no missed opportunities. The old adage of "if you love it, set it free" applies here. Whatever is truly yours will return to you. Don't let stagnation hold you back, move on and trust that life will get better.

Balance

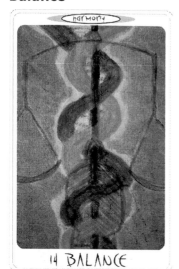

14 BALANCE

Keyword: Harmony
Chakra: Throat, Light-Blue

The symbols of DNA and the scales are used to convey the idea of a mixture that is in flux and wants to achieve balance. This card is usually called 'temperance' which is supposed to conceptually convey the ideas of balance and moderation, but in our society it has unfortunately become associated with guilt because of the Temperance Movement, so to universalize the nomenclature, the words 'harmony' and 'balance' are used instead of 'temperance.'

The 'Temperance Society' formed in 1835 was Catholic in origin and advocated teetotalism and abstinence rather than moderation in all things. This rather extreme group resurfaced in the 1920's, and their reign resulted in the debauchery created by prohibition during the 1930's. This is the legacy of the word 'temperance.'

So, we'll use the terms *moderation*, *harmony* and *balance* to convey the meaning of the card. Moderation is germane in most moral behavior models. It is held as one of the four virtues in Hellenic society, one of the five precepts of Buddhism, and one of the key tenets of Christianity and Hinduism. Moderation in practice means curtailing the passions in favor of reason. So when this card appears in a reading, outside spiritual forces are reminding us to control our behavior in favor of the balanced path.

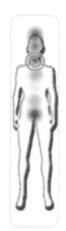

When we first learn to walk, we have trouble retaining our balance. As we grow we are not only expected to balance our bodies, but our social activities, our work life, our home life and our emotions. Sometimes all of this balancing can take its toll, and we need to recalibrate our inner ear which is our center of balance in our bodies. By inner ear here, I mean our inner spiritual ear and that simply means we need to listen internally to our intuition and find the best way to strike a balance in our lives. Being in balance doesn't mean giving up our passions, nor does it mean giving up reason. Like the mountain pose in yoga, when we get this card we are being challenged to both relax and to pay attention at the same time. Relaxed concentration is only achievable when we are in balance. When we are in balance we have an inner knowing, a way of observing that is beyond the five senses. When we are in balance we are in harmony with nature right down to the molecular bindings of our DNA. This is a state that is difficult to maintain. Meditation, yoga and being outdoors are all ways of getting back into a state of harmony. But doing too much meditation, yoga or any activity will still lead you to being out of sorts. Listening to your body is the first step towards renewing your balance.

Reversed: Obviously you are out of balance. Maybe you've become too passionate about some aspect of your life and you need to tone it down a bit, or it could be you're working too hard in some area of your life. When you get the Balance card reversed it usually is a signal to slow down and relax. You need to recalibrate and listen to your inner self. You could probably use some quiet time alone to recalibrate what you hold dear. Focus on bringing calm back into your life. Or you may need to do some reenergizing by doing a little bit of yoga. One pose that isn't difficult to do, if you can stand, is the mountain. To do the pose you simply stand with both feet placed firmly on the floor. Stand straight but not straining at attention, and look forward. If you can't stand you can still visualize a mountain and think of yourself as becoming the mountain. The idea is that a mountain is easy with itself, it doesn't rush and it is always in harmony with its surroundings. If it quakes, so does the earth around it. If it erupts, it is because great energy is flowing through it. But mostly mountains are silent and seem eternal. When you do the mountain pose, the idea is to identify with the majesty of the earth and to recognize your inner balance at the core of your being.

The Devil

15 DEVIL - obsession

Keyword: Disrespect
Chakra: Root, Red

Materialism, identifying too much with your corporeal body, possession, and obsession (lust) are associated with this card. Separation from humanity, from spirit and source, or higher brain functions like compassion and logic is also implied. When the Devil appears in a spread it means identifying more with the physical body than with the spirit, and acting from your lower chakras rather than your higher ones.

You may be fixated or obsessed with something. Under the devil's influence we tend to seek externally for fulfillment or gratification. We want to succeed by any means necessary or at the expense of others. We are being controlled by the baser aspects of the human condition. In this image, a man stands along a highway lined with human skulls. His red face mask indicates a demon symbol in Chinese lore and also represents blood sacrifice. The Jackal shadow notes the duality of man and beast. In Jungian terms, the man represents 'the Shadow' or the aspects of self that are unconscious, rejected, repressed, or undeveloped, both good and bad. We create the world in our own image. Our inner states of consciousness are mirrored in daily situations. If we want to live in a giving, peaceful world then we must become giving and peaceful. If we feel like fate keeps handing us a stacked deck, then we should look at the significance of these repeating patterns, and try changing our thoughts. We all have a Shadow, and confronting the Shadow is essential for self awareness. If we continue to disregard the Shadow with "why me" thoughts, then we are going to attract the Shadow through the mirrors of other people. Work with the Shadow and recognize it for what it is: human impulses that require discipline to control.

Although not used for this deck, often a horned half-man/half-goat is used to represent the Devil. Many pagan symbols eventually combined to create the archetype of what we think of when we say 'the devil'. Whether it was the Greek Bacchus/Pan with the 'frivolous' rites of spring, or Sumerian Zu stealing the 'Tablets of Destiny' or 'Satan-ikas,' the founder of a small sect of Jains in India who painted their faces red and wore red robes - these, along with numerous other images were co-opted and ridiculed or demonized to strengthen the Catholic Church's political standing in the Middle Ages. The oppression of the devil is still present and influencing our world daily. Look no farther than *The Devil Came on Horse-back,*[14] the documentary film by Brian Steidle, an American who went to Sudan in 2004 to observe the ceasefire between southern Sudan and the gov-ernment in the north. Steidle ended up witnessing the genocide that was just starting in Darfur. The word *Janjaweed* refers to "devils on horseback" which is the Arab militia. They are trained, armed, and funded by the central government to ethnically cleanse Darfur. Let's begin to work with the Shadow, recognize it and bring it into the light, one thought at a time.

Reversed: The first step is recognizing our role in our own bondage. To free ourselves from the internal turmoil of circular thinking or obsessive behavior we must first analyze the situation and recognize the triggers that create the response. When we are feeling dull, bored, or trapped in a situation, we are not using our higher mind processes. Like Pavlov's dogs who responded to the ringing of a bell, we too have built-in responses to situational stimuli. If you find yourself in a situation that you don't like, figure out how you are attracting the 'shadow' self. Try to find a new response, if not in actual deed, then in thought. In other words, say to yourself "next time I'll do it this way..." and complete the action in as much detail as you can in your thoughts. The Devil in reverse is just as insidious as the Devil right-side-up; the difference is found in how much you acknowledge or block your role in the situation. Think of your thoughts as your children or little images of yourself. Focus on each separately and acknowledge your base responses to things like need, lust, desire, want, fear, or sadness. Once you have them clearly in mind, surround them with your higher responses of love, understanding, acceptance, and forgiveness. Now create a new scenario in your mind of how you will respond the next time the problem occurs. You will find that the actual response you desire will come easier next time.

The Tower

Keyword: Destruction
Chakra: Solar Plexus, Yellow

Unconsciously inspired by 9/11 but still using conventional Tarot, this card employs the symbolism of the hanged man falling off a tall building. The meaning of the Tower card is destruction of preconceived notions about who you are and why you are here. Think of the Biblical tower of Babel and you have the general notion of the card. Enlightenment is forced upon us by ripping away idle beliefs that have no bearing on our spiritual reality.

Self-understanding and knowledge are destroyed, or obliterated, and who you thought you were falls away. You are reevaluating, and that allows you to find innocence again. When you get this card in a reading, know that a fresh start is at hand.

The eye above the buildings represents omniscience. The buildings are the beliefs we build up about ourselves in the world. In a momentary flash of clarity we understand every-thing, and then it is gone, and so is the understanding of ourselves. In Hinduism it is referred to as the 'sarv-gyaata' moment.

The understanding may leave us as quickly as it came – a flash of insight. We'll probably feel a blow to the ego in some way, or we may be left feeling utterly destroyed, but at the same time knowing that we are getting a second chance to rebuild, renew and start anew.

The eye also represents the opening of the psychic inner eye at the brow chakra, but because it is so devastating to have our beliefs about ourselves forcibly changed, the solar plexus chakra of self power is where we feel the energy strike. A sick stomach feeling may give way to weakness. Al-low yourself the space to heal. Sleep and acknowledging the change will help you.

Allegorically, in the hero's journey, the sacrifice made by the hanged man is not in vain if he has faced his fears of death and replaced his understanding of death with the belief in his own renewal. He must pass through his inner hell and replace his internal devil's ego with balance. When he arrives at the tower he will feel the final shock of revelation about his own true nature, and he will be ready for robust renewal.

Reversed: You may not be ready to accept your power or the change that is happening to you as real. You may be looking to others to solve problems that are actually intrinsic to your own nature. When you get the Tower reversed, you have been building with blocks that have prevented you from seeing the situation as it really is. Building blocks are a great resource for knowledge, or self-esteem, but sometimes they get in the way of our seeing our true inner landscape. The tower isn't easy – it is about upheaval of inner understanding. You may need to let go of someone or something to move ahead emotionally, physically or spiritually, and trying to hold on will only make things worse. If you can let go, then take the plunge and do so. The time is now because change is inevitable, and this is a huge change.

The Star

Keyword: Inspiration
Chakra: Crown, Violet

> *Star light, star bright,*
> *The first star I see tonight,*
> *I wish I may, I wish I might,*
> *Have the wish I wish tonight.*

As a glyph, stars define something of distinction. When we call someone a "star," it is because they have reminded us of our divinity. They have communicated something we're all familiar with, and they have helped us key into the truth about human nature's vulnerability and power. When you get the Star card, hope and healing are forming around you. Peace, serenity and emotional clearing reveal the path to a newly inspired you. You are a star, what you do is inspirational and helps heal the planet. Be inspired because when we are inspired, we feel reborn; we are capable of great feats of strength and love.

The stars in the night sky inspire and empower us; seeing them creates a feeling of serenity and endless possibility. Ultimately the Star card is about hope for the future. Receiving it inspires peace and trust. When you get the Star, you're being reminded of your divinity. Transformation and emotional release create room for joy and love. Express your inner star power by letting go of all the misconceptions, shame, guilt, anger and sadness that you may have been holding onto. Accept joy, serenity and love as your guides as you redefine yourself as a person of distinction. Cherish your ability to inspire others, and help them to find their own inner light. Share the night sky with the world. Look up and be inspired.

The five-sided star represents the energy of the four elements (earth, air, fire and water,) and the inspiration of the spirit or 'soul' of man is the final point. Typically, in the Star Tarot the woman in the card is thought to be a Naiad, or a river nymph, and akin to the temperance card, she sifts the

71

waters of life. In the White Light Tarot deck, the star dances to the hum of the eternal bees. Her arc creates the beginning of the sacred geometry that will take her to the cosmos. The Star card using Homer's iconography according to Porphyry's interpretation (1518) celebrates the descent of the soul into the world and its return to God and the immortals.

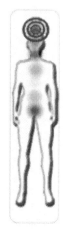

Reversed: You may be feeling uninspired and too earthbound. To put it bluntly, your inner couch potato is showing. You're behaving in a discordant manner, so you've disconnected from possibility. You aren't seeing the hope in a situation, or maybe you've chosen to ignore the possibilities which are right there in front of you.

Whatever it is that is going on, when you get the star reversed it means a conscious refusal to see the good that is right ahead. Cynicism, pessimism and depression are taking over the situation, making it impossible to feel inspired. Boredom is just a diluted form of anger, so find a way of breaking free and inspire yourself by inspiring others. When you actively engage in pursuing your dreams you inspire others and create room for inner beauty to blossom. Let go of your guilt, anger, shame and be who you really are — an inspiring being of knowledge and light.

The Moon

Keyword: Flow
Chakra: Sacral, Orange

Our journey through life involves change and phases. Understanding, revelation and knowledge come in stages both conscious and subconscious. The moon governs the subconscious information surfacing through dreams and intuition, but because of its association with sub-conscious knowledge, it is also associated with illusion. In many decks the moon is considered a bad omen, due to a complex cultural clash of Pagan and Christian beliefs, as well as the phasing of the moon (read: changeable nature) and its association with illusion (subconscious). Therefore the moon is associated with trust, or lack of trust.

This is one of the cards whose negative interpretation I have always disagreed with. I feel the moon is a wonderful symbol of companionship; after all it is earth's satellite. The moon is also a symbol of motherhood, as her belly grows full each month, and it is a symbol of wealth and purity for her pearl-like glow.

If we view the moon as feminine in nature, we connect her with flow, as in the tides, moods, menstrual cycles, sea harvests, and even changes in the stock market. The moon is our natural time keeper, and the word 'month' comes from the word 'moon.' From new moon to full moon is a time of new beginnings, a time when thought is swift and quick. Dreams may seem more intense and since subconscious thought is most developed at the dark of the moon, psychic abilities come more easily. On the other hand, the waning lunar cycle from full to dark is the time to get rid of those aspects of your life you no longer want. This is the time to quit smoking, or to start a weight loss program. Feel the pulse and rhythm the moon conveys. Trust the flow and phases of your life. The cycles of the moon remind us that change is natural and that life consists of a series of phases. Call down the moon to bear witness to your transformation.

Interestingly, in most ancient Indo-European cultures, the moon is associated with a male god, including the Sumerian (Nannar), Hindu (Chandra and Shiva), Egyptian (Thoth and Osiris) and Norse (Mani). Expressions and stories like "the old man in the moon," and "the cow jumped over the moon" come from ancient beliefs and rituals.

But in the White Light Tarot interpretation, the Moon is associated with the goddess. In the cultures that favor the feminine view of the moon's influence, she is associated with growth, wealth, grace, beauty, femininity, nurturing and immortality. In the Greek pantheon the moon is associated with Apollo and Selene, in the Roman guise Luna, or Diana, and among Celtic deities she is called Mona; for the Tibetan pantheon Mana, and Chinese, Chang-Ngo.

If you get this card and you are in a difficult place, trust that this is only a phase. Change is on the horizon. Accept that your inner transformation is real because paradoxically change is the only thing we can count on. "Change is the only constant," as the saying goes. When you get the moon card in a spread, it's probably a good time to find out what phase the moon is in and do some meditation under the moonlight. When the moon is waxing, or growing, (looks like a 'D,') concentrate on the things you want to increase in your life, like love, health and wealth. If the moon looks like a 'C' then it has just passed full and it's waning, or diminishing. This is the time to meditate on those influences you want to decrease, like overindulgence or self-recrimination. When the moon is full, bask in its glow and give thanks to the wonder that life offers us. Breathe in her serenity and fill yourself with peace.

Reversed: It's a phase. Plain and simple, that is what this card is saying. You may feel under-the-influence in some way, a little bit loony. The illusion is that the state we're in is permanent. The Moon helps remind us that this state of being is an illusion and what is going on is just a phase, nothing more. "Wait and see," the Moon is saying. Reflect on your influence and that of those closest to you in your life. Release the attachment to outcomes. Whether they're good or bad it doesn't matter – it is just a phase. Change is good, and we should trust that everything will change for the better. We need to trust in our decisions, which allow us to change, as ultimately that is what being alive is all about.

The Sun

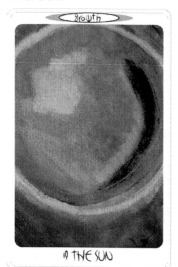

Keyword: Growth
Chakra: Sacral, Orange

The Sun rekindles our power to burn through to the heart of the matter, which leads to growth. Without growth we cannot survive, any more than the earth can survive without the sun. In older cultures, the sun is the mother figure. Think of the Egyptian goddess Hathor, Mat, and Sekhmet with the head of a lioness, or the sun disk captured between her horns in her headdress. Think of the Norse goddess Saewelô, written as a rune S or $\mathsf{\zeta}$. In the Norse pantheon she is also called Sunna or Sol and she brings the sunrise with her chariot. Or think of Celtic goddess Macha, her unbridled strength fearsome to men. In Japan she is Amaterasu. She is fierce, joyful, and loyal. She is often a healer and warrior at the same time, and she is the protector of growing things.

The Sun, the Wheel of Fortune and the Chariot iconography are similar and linked as a power triad.[15] Among the Balts, the connection between the sun and spinning is very old, and the sun-stone, amber, forms the link. Sometimes amber discs were also placed in the grave, perhaps as prayers to the Sun Goddess to spin forth the lost life in another body.... "[A]mber was considered a magical substance for a spinner; as the light never tangles in the sky, so an amber spindle protected the new thread from snarls caused by unhappy or malicious spirits."

Saule, my amber weeping Goddess
creating light like thread.
As "Saules Mat" my mother sun, daily blessing
your thankful world with light.[16]

The word *chakra* translates to "spinning wheels of light," so if you think of the sun as our universe's solar plexus chakra, you can see what power it offers us to burn away illusion. For the White Light Tarot's Sun card, the chakra connection is to the sacral chakra or sex center. This is because of the strong connection to the creative source. The sacral center is the source of our growth and creativity, and because of the association with the goddess and growth, my inclination was to place it with the sacral chakra. However, you may also want to use the Sun card in meditation in connection with the solar plexus. To quote Wayne Dyer, "When you dance, your purpose is not to get to a certain place  on the floor. It's to enjoy each step along the way. That's what life is. There's no way to happiness. Happiness is the way. It's what you bring to life." Be like the sun and know that you can shine all day long, and burn through anything.

Reversed: If the Sun is reversed, you may be experiencing a cloudy feeling. Feeling dull, dark, baked, overdone, you may be trying too hard to get things going that you really don't care about. Your sacral center may be out of alignment. It could be overstimulated, but usually when we get a reversed card, it is an indicator of blocked energy. Assuming that when you get this card, there is some blockage of self esteem, sexual energy or creativity, you may need to do some clearing in this area. Going out into the sun will help. If you can't go out, then try placing a glass of water in the sunshine. Allow the water to absorb the energy and then drink the water. This may help you clear away some of the blocks to your continued growth. Vitamin D and/or fortified milk may help, not only for the symbolic links to mother and growth but for the literal health connection as well.

Vitamin D3 is produced in skin exposed to sunlight. It plays an important role in the maintenance of organ systems, it promotes bone formation, it inhibits parathyroid hormone secretion and it affects the immune system by promoting immunosuppressant, phagocytosis, and anti-tumor activity. A vitamin D deficiency can result in conditions that impair conversion of vitamin D into active metabolites, such as liver or kidney disorders. It can also lead to bone softening diseases like rickets in children and osteomalacia in adults, and possibly contributes to osteoporosis. Research has indicated that vitamin D deficiency is linked to colon cancer.[17]

When you get the Sun card reversed, try to get some sun. Joy and growth are blocked, so find ways to plant seeds.

Awakening

2⁰ ΛѰΛΚΕΝΙΝᏀ

Keyword: Enlightenment
Chakra: Brow, Indigo

Also known as the Judgment card, the Awakening card is about epiphany. An epiphany is "a sudden intuitive leap of understanding, especially through an ordinary but striking occurrence."[18] Similar to waking from a dream with a sudden realization, an epiphany is like awakening from your life to realize that the possibilities are endless. Synchronicity plays a key role when you get this card, so stay alert. Enlightenment is being at the threshold of clarity and maintaining that clarity. You are lightening your load, literally. You may experience a heightening of your sensory perceptions. You have been judged and you are now re-deemed - the past falls away, you have no regrets, no fear, no doubt, the moment is now: *carpe diem* (seize the day). You suddenly understand.

The White Light Tarot deck's Awakening card is about understanding the way of the bodhisattva. Without effort you are able to attain peace. Compassion and peace are the states of the bodhisattva. When we achieve this state, we have a clarity that allows us to understand what motivates us and others to do what we do. We actively choose to live well regardless of circumstance. Living well encompasses discipline without effort. We act from our center of bliss and joy, and continually do the right thing at the right time. You have passed through constraint of judgment into enlightened behavior. Living well means caring for yourself, others, and the planet with all of your attention, and living in the moment. Continue to evolve until you never need to remind yourself of your own worth, the value of oth-

ers, or that the best course of actions is always a peaceful center of compassion.

When you get this card, a time of rebirth is at hand. You understand your inner calling, you have accepted past mistakes and you've released and cleared any lingering repression. This is a card of absolution, reconciliation, forgiveness and salvation. Follow your heart and undertake to do your best, but also know that this state is difficult for most of us to maintain. Remember who you truly are and maintain your connection to the ascended masters whom you now emulate.

Reversed: You're not paying close enough attention. The signs are there showing you the way home, but all you are aware of is feeling judged. When you get this card you're not awake. You're in a mesmerized zombie state, unable to awaken to what you can do to make a difference in your life and the lives of others. This world is only a portion of what makes up reality; don't get too caught up in materialism. When you get this card there is something that you're denying in yourself that is arresting the energy flow. Develop your ability to feel compassion for others, and eventually you may feel it for yourself as well. Compassion is not the same feeling as love or pity. It comes from a deep knowing that we are all the same, that we are all connected, that we are all one. If you are having trouble understanding or feeling compassion, find something you can relate to that isn't a human being. It could be a pet, a tree, a river, a computer, a book, a jelly mold, whatever it is, take the feeling you have for it and apply it to the rest of your life. It should be a feeling of peace and satisfaction, a feeling that there is no reason to change that thing because it is perfect the way it is. Now endeavor to feel that with everyone you meet and when you look in the mirror, and you'll be on your way to the bodhisattva state of full awakening.

The Universe

21 THE UNIVERSE

Keyword: Divine Light
Chakra: Crown, Violet

The Universe is pure mind, universal consciousness, energy. You have successfully tapped into source energy and cosmic matter has manifested into form. Ashes to ashes, and dust to dust - a cycle is complete. With a sigh of fulfillment, you can now walk from the inward spiral path through the doorway or "eye of the needle" into the outward spiral. All of the other high arcana states of mind have led up to this one. Innocence leads to experience, experience leads to understanding, and understanding leads to communicating what you have discovered. You are at home anywhere and with anyone, because the universe is your home. Getting this card indicates in some way that you have arrived and that you know the satisfaction of being complete.

You've passed through all the phases of a project or life phase. From enthusiasm to winning support to the trials and tribulations of the tasks, through the doubts and missteps, you have emerged with the knowledge. You've sealed the deal, so rest up and celebrate your achievements. When you call upon the universe for support, support is given. Now that the cycle is completed, you may rest easy, but recognize that the journey is a circle, and you're right back where you started, soon to become the fool with a new task or life phase to master.

Reversed: You're not connecting to your potential the way you'd like, perhaps. The problem isn't your lack of skill, talent, intelligence or likability; it is your lack of trust and faith in yourself, others, and the universal law of

81

attraction that is holding you back. You can achieve your dreams with the proper enthusiasm supported by fortitude and fairness. If the world has got you down, then maybe it is time to put the brakes on what you're doing and try another approach. Everything will become clear in its own time, and when you get back in synch with the world, you'll remember just how much you have going for you. In the meantime, slow down, back off and wait. Clear away the clutter and start to form the big picture of what you really want to manifest in your life. Let the universe do what it does by answering the call, but you must do the inner work necessary to stay clear and focused on your dreams. Don't let others dissuade you from being your authentic self. When you are authentic, you shine, and the universe is on your side.

3

THE SWORDS

The swords represent ideals, intellect, logic, breath and wind; theirs is the element of air. Thought is the essence of the realm of the sword because of its shining speed, lightening-fast strike, and cutting clarity. It is appropriate that the lesser arcana start with this suit because this is not so much a suit of physical action as one of decisive thought. If thought is action in meditation, right before manifestation, then the swords are an artistic representation of a state of mind right before the action occurs. As the synapse fires, so strikes the sword. Then the mists part, and clarity of purpose and knowledge is found. Air circulates and motivates us to move with it. When the swords strike us we become swept up in the moment. In anticipation of an action, we hold our breath, and when we finally breathe that sigh of relief, the demands are over. We have landed where we are supposed to be.

The King of Swords

Keyword: High Ideals
Chakra: Sacral, Orange

The King of Swords lives by high ideals. He wants you to think his way. In essence he is a proselytizer, but not in the religious sense. He'll talk until he is blue in the face making sure that you understood the finer points of his argument. He is a great storyteller and philosopher, erudite and intellectually intimidating. He is a go-getter, a type-A personality, and doggedly he'll get things done. He is not easy to satisfy, yet he is not a man of hasty actions.

Never bored, the King of Swords is intelligent, intellectual, and a just ruler; he is ruled by the mind and refuses to be swayed by the heart. He offers compassion with an edge, so to speak. If you are in need, he is the great protector for the downtrodden, and he can make an excellent advisor in legal or financial matters.

In the White Light Tarot image, the King of Swords stands amongst rock crystal. Our hero has a huge sword in front of his open heart which is beating raw against the hilt. Symbolically, the King of Swords has torn down the edifice of obfuscation with his sword of clarity. He makes use of his intellect, and expects the same of those closest to him. He is a man of science and technology, capable of physical prowess and intimidation. He does not rule with his heart, but with his head. He is not particularly in touch with his emotions, so it may take him longer than usual to understand his emotional responses to certain situations. Be patient with him. The King of Swords needs help understanding his feminine side. He has trouble relating to the feminine, and thinks of it as "other." Rational, cool and collected under fire, he can blow through things that he perceives as details. The King of

Swords makes a good lawyer or teacher, but don't forget to pass in your homework on time. No excuses will suffice.

Reversed: Logic has turned against the King of Swords and what remains is arrogance that has changed into megalomania. His wit slices and dices as he changes from a forthright and just man into a craven manipulator. He has lost his way and pits his wit against all takers, not for truth or justice, but simply because he can. Do not take him on in this condition. He craves power and has delusions of grandeur. He criticizes to assert his dominance, but his authority lacks conviction as it is founded more upon self-loathing than anything else. Recognize that he is clinging to an outmoded way of thinking, and that he'll need a push to change. If he can catch a glimpse of himself in another, perhaps he'll change back into the moral, practical, capable man he used to be.

The Queen of Swords

QUEEN OF SWORDS

Keyword: Beauty
Chakra: Crown, Violet

The Queen of Swords is a woman of poise, distinction, and conscience. She has at her side a swan. The swan symbolizes light, femininity, and intuition, but the swan is also an emblem of power and transformation. In Norse mythology, the Valkyries morphed into swans when they swooped into battle to lead the fallen warriors to Valhalla. Zeus seduced Leda when he shape-shifted into a great swan, and Leda gave birth to Helen of Troy "the face that launched a thousand ships" during the Trojan War.

The swan is also an alchemical symbol of the marriage of opposites, and possibly a hermaphrodic nature. At its crux, there is a mixture of light and dark in this card that is hard to disassociate. The Queen holds her sword balanced, ready for up-stroke or down-stroke. She represents intellectual perfection and beauty, but her power is in her perception. She can transform what seems ugly into something splendid. Her actions are acute and precise, as are her decisions. When you get the Queen of Swords, allow her to help you see the inner beauty in yourself and others. She can help you transform your intuition and balance your emotions.

Reversed: Beauty has become vanity. Intuition has become suspicion. When the Queen of Swords is reversed, you or someone close to you is being defensive, intolerant and overly discriminating. The Queen of Swords represents sorrow because she is too caught up in minutia to see the big picture. Her sharp, complex mind is racing. Too headstrong and not thinking clearly, she is ready to accuse, to blame and seemingly to face things head on, but actually she isn't. She may seem ready for the fight of her life, but she's quite vulnerable because of her agitated state.

As an analogy, think of the Queen of Swords in the forest (earth) which isn't her element. She can't see the forest for the trees, so she assumes every tree is an obstacle that is testing her, something to be conquered. So she stands at the foot of the tree, frozen and frustrated, unwilling to go around the tree, trying to will the tree out of the way. When you get this card, know that you or someone close to you may need to back off from the situation. Every tree is not an obstacle. To see the path, you have to change your thinking or your point of view. Turn around and you see the greater forest. If she would just look up, she'd see her element air, and feel a bit clearer and a little less frustrated and like her old capable self.

We can find a path around any obstacle, but we have to quit panicking and blaming others. It can be difficult to do, but if we're willing to wait and become calm, a path will emerge in the forest of doubt and frustration. Then we'll finally see that the trees are part of a large, green, wonderful forest, and that the forest is only part of the interconnected web of the world.

The Knight of Swords

Keyword: Duty
Chakra: Solar Plexus, Yellow

The Knight of Swords is the epitome of devotion and duty. This card inclines noble pursuits that lead to concrete actions. Idealism tempered by realism and working within the system for the betterment of all, that is the charge of the Knight of Swords.

He is not one to back down from a challenge, nor is he dissuaded from mediation. You'll find him working in places like Doctors without Borders, The Animal Rescue League, and Habitat for Humanity, or in homeless shelters and first response units. He is a motivated motivator. He believes in working to better society and in the innate goodness of people, and he finds that the proof is in the pudding.

The Knight of Swords has some of the qualities of King Arthur. As a mythical figure, Arthur represents our ideals, yet he may have been a real man. New evidence has led investigators to connect the legend of Arthur with a tribe of Iranians called the Sarmatians. Interestingly, this tribe's altar was a sword in a stone. The Arthurian legend is where we get our ideas about knights and chivalry, and though there isn't a definitive list of manners, the seven virtues and a list from chivalrytoday.com is a good place to start. Courage, justice, mercy, generosity, faith, nobility, and hope are the primary virtues of chivalry. When you get this card, you or someone close to you is acting with great faith in humanity. Have faith and fealty in what you are doing and stay the course. Call upon the Knight of Swords to cut any cords that bind you to negative thinking. It is his duty to serve, and he is devoted to your cause.

Reversed: Are you shirking your responsibilities and du-
ties? The ideals that you seek do exist. Find a way to
demonstrate your ideals and bring them out in yourself. No
one is perfect in their actions; we are perfect at our core, but
we are human, and sometimes our reactions don't live up to
our ideals of how we see ourselves. That's okay because
we're here to learn, and we'll do better next time. The King of
Swords reversed is just a reminder that we must still strive to
live up to our ideals. He's there to lend you a hand when you
fall on your *arse*; he'll pick you up and set you right. Don't
worry, he's behind you one hundred percent, and he knows
you're trying your best. His message is one of encouragement. "Face the battle," he says, "but if you're outnumbered
then find a place to hole up and heal." He is not going to let
you get out of doing your duty however, so if there is some
facing up to a task or feelings to be done, he is there to gently but firmly nudge you along.

Page of Swords

PAGE of SWORDS

Keyword: Message
Chakra: Throat, Light-Blue
Akin to Hermes, the messenger of the gods, this messenger is masked. He is known as a *hermeneus*, an interpreter who can bridge boundaries. Hermes gave us the art and science of "hermeneutics," which is essentially the art of interpretation. When we seek to understand our hidden inner experience or we try to understand something from another's point of view, we are engaging in hermeneutics. To reveal the truth, the Page of Swords wears a mask for our protection, for what he may say and how the truth appears to us may be too harsh, bright or fantastic for us to understand. He communicates the truth in the best possible way for us to comprehend his meaning, with peace, light and loving intensions. He is urging necessary changes from within that will carry you to the next vibratory level. He is revealing what you already know, if you'll only search your soul and listen to his message.

Like the players at the masked ball, he is interested in connecting with the real inner you, and not the exterior edifice that may or may not reflect your true inner beauty. Give way to your ability to practice hermeneutics, or the art of interpreting hidden meaning. When you get this card, it means you should allow yourself to hear and see the messages that come to you throughout the day. Maybe it's a feather floating by, or a penny in the street; maybe it's a bird song noticed over the din of the city, or maybe it's this card reading. Whatever it is that takes your attention for a moment, honor that as extraordinary and as a hidden message from the Page of Swords. If nothing else, use these messages as a spiritual booster, and let the flow of loving messages from the universe filter through.

Reversed: The Page of Swords is an emissary, an envoy, an agent of change. He holds a mask to his face, representing that the change or message comes from within. When you get the Page of Swords reversed, it means you are not yet aware of the internal change in attitude or spiritual understanding that is taking place. Understand this is not something that is seen on the surface; this is something that happens in dreams, in imagery and symbolism. The message, like the messenger, is disguised. When you look back on this time later, the connections that led you here will be clear, and you'll realize that growth was inevitable. Change is good, welcome it.

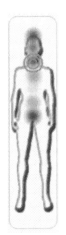

Ten of Swords

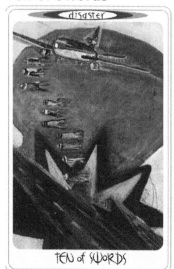

TEN of SWORDS

Keyword: Disaster
Chakra: Root, Red

This card is a clear departure from the standard Tarot imagery for the Ten of Swords, but I believe it imparts the meaning of the card more clearly for modern users. Ten bombs are being dropped over a target. The saying "you dropped a bomb on me" comes to mind, and the notion of overkill is demonstrated. War is the escalation of hostilities brought about by economic or political insecurities. When this card appears, know that the peace process will be difficult to achieve because, in some measure, you're fostering a hostile environment, and if you don't come to an accord, chances are good that more battles will ensue. War is rarely the answer to our problems. We all have our triggers, but we don't have to act like Pavlov's dogs, giving in to the prompt. We are thinking and feeling human beings and generally people are compassionate, so let's act accordingly. Think before you act. When you get the Ten of Swords, you might need to walk a mile in the other guy's shoes, or you might need to walk away. In any event you should show a little compassion. For some reason you've come off as insensitive. Reacting too quickly can give way to acting defensively. Try understanding your opponent's point of view to lessen any feeling of misunderstanding, fear, hostility and failure. Acknowledging the feelings involved doesn't mean that you've sanctioned the behavior. You can forgive the person without forgiving the action, and sometimes that is enough to move from a standstill to progressive understanding.

Usually, the Ten of Swords pictographically is either ten crisscrossed swords or the image of a man stabbed in the back by ten swords on a lonely beach. In my estimation, the conventional Tarot image is similar to Jean-Louis David's work, *The Death of Marat*, painted in 1793. The painting was a political statement to be sure, not only relative to the fact that the painting was rendered to avenge the death of Marat at the time, but also due to the fact that the graphic nature of the image led to political upheaval. "In 1795, it was removed from the meeting hall of the Deputies by a decree forbidding the public display of any portrait whose subject had not been dead for at least ten years." (*The History of Art*, H.W. Janson) Culturally, we've lost that political context in the conventional Tarot image, so White Light Tarot endeavors to recapture and communicate the feeling of political upheaval, helplessness, and fear that the Ten of Swords should engender.

Hence, the Ten of Swords becomes the Ten of Bombs. War leading to nuclear genocide is one of human society's most devastating threats. It is unique to modern consciousness. This Ten of Swords indicates that too much mental activity has led to despair and hostility. When you get the Ten of Swords in a reading, know that facing your greatest fear with compassion will make you stronger. Fear forces us to gather all of our strength together and face down whatever threatens us. Tired though we may be, we carry on, and if we face our threats with compassion, we may create an ally. Whether what we face is a failure in ourselves, in a situation, or something else, humiliation stings, but it also points out our frail humanity, and offers us a chance to practice compassion. Peace and forgiveness are the hallmarks of a mature spirit. Forgive yourself, forgive others, plant seeds of peace, and they will grow.

Reversed: When you get the Ten of Swords reversed, the meaning is essentially the same, but you may be feeling that you are the victim of hostilities rather than an active participant. It doesn't matter, even if that is true. When you play the victim role, you set up the energy for abuse. You must act with compassion and find a way to bridge the gap, acting as neither victim nor perpetrator. You need only to forgive the person, not the action they have taken against you.

Nine of Swords

NINE of SWORDS

Keyword: Vulnerable
Chakra: Crown, Violet

Mental cruelty, pride, conflict, and politics, in this case meaning taking on a group mentality rather than thinking for oneself, creates problems for us. Without self-confidence, continuous internal and external power struggles ensue. White Light Tarot's image is a departure from conventional Tarot imagery and idiom, as it is drawn from a still capture of Toshiaki Toyoda's 2001 Film, *Blue Spring (Aoi haru)*.[19]

Blue Spring examines the power dynamics of a group of teenage boys as they struggle to prove themselves. For youth culture, the film is a valid social commentary on the grim reality that once locked in a peer-pressure dynamic, there is no way to escape without alienation. In the film, the tormented become the tormentors, as through various rites of passage, all participants perpetuate the cycle of brooding and suffering.

When you get this card, you (or whomever the card represents) are demonstrating a dependence on cruelty or despondency. Aloof and detached behavior mutes intense feelings of anguish and despair, which are only relieved by behaving brutally.

The Nine of Swords image depicts the boys as the actual swords; each is a double edged blade, capable of great heartlessness. Alone in his thoughts, each boy is conflicted and about to participate in a death-defying challenge to become leader of the gang. Each in turn will hang off of the roof's railing and clap his hands one more time than his opponent, and if he is not quick enough he will plummet to his death on the concrete below.

When thoughts gang up on us they are a formidable force that is difficult to thwart. The boys in Nine of Swords represent a downward spiral, one that is associated with group mentality like that of *Blue Spring*, or for that matter, *Lord of the Flies*.[20] Alone, even in a group, the Nine of Swords is about the anguish we feel when we cannot gain the acceptance that we crave.

In order to stop the torment of a tortured mind you will need to forgive yourself and those around you. Find a way to lift yourself away from the need for external approval. Try writing everything down that is disagreeable in your life and performing a ritual to release it, burning the paper, flushing it down the toilet, casting it out to sea, burying it, leaving it on the subway for someone to find, whatever seems appropriate. Release yourself from the cycle of brooding and torment; don't jump off the roof, it will prove nothing. Find a way to accept joy back into your life again. You'll know you're releasing when you can see the beauty in a painting or a flower without pain, hear music without experiencing heartache, and eat and sleep without fear or worry. When you get this card, it is time to do something nice so that you'll feel nice without the need of outside approval. Approve of yourself just the way you are, and let go of anguish.

Reversed Anger and resentment may be hidden, and you are trying to practice tolerance, but manipulative behavior will not help in overcoming feelings of inadequacy or superiority. Pretending to be tolerant may seem to lead to acceptance, but it really only leads to separation from one's true self. Don't allow yourself to be manipulated, and don't manipulate others for political gain. Be true to yourself, examine who you are, and stand up for your ideals. Eventually, you'll find others who will accept you gladly for who you really are. If you need to adjust your thinking to be more inclusive, or more tolerant, then find ways of being less judgmental. One definition of tolerance is "a fair, objective, and permissive attitude toward opinions and practices that differ from one's own." In order to accept others and appreciate their differences, you have to accept yourself and value your own differences, so start there and don't try to change others; try to change yourself.

Eight of Swords

EIGHT OF SWORDS

Keyword: Afraid
Chakra: Heart, Green

Poor little one, indecision grips your heart making it hard to breathe. The Eight of Swords is an image of a beating heart with icicles stabbing painfully into it. Fear has stopped you in your tracks. You've hesitated like a deer in the headlights, and if you don't move soon, you'll get hit.

When we're afraid to make a final decision, the pain can be overwhelming. We feel uncertain because we're afraid that we might make the wrong choice, or we'll regret our decision later. Vacillation saps our energy, making it impossible to evaluate the best course of action. When this happens, consider stepping out of harm's way, letting traffic pass by, and babying yourself until you're calm. Allow yourself a little space to put aside the actual decision. Create scenarios in your mind that have various outcomes. Which one resonates with you the most? Which do you like the best? Do they lead to the same result or vastly different results? You may feel powerless right now, or feel there is no way out of a situation, but that is never the case. It may be painful, but you always have a choice. You can decide to take the necessary steps to change your circumstances.

The icicles will melt away and you'll be able to breathe deep. Your heart still beats, though wounded. All wounds heal with time. Baby yourself to make sure your wounds heal thoroughly. You deserve the best, as we all do. But remember, we reap what we sow. Pay attention to planting seeds for the highest good possible. Till the soil of your mind, and don't allow the seeds of doubt, fear and indecision to root, or you'll lose the abundant fertile soil to weeds.

Reversed: A poor decision can have a domino effect, knocking down everything that you thought was stable in your life. The Eight of Swords reversed points out that just because the dominos fell doesn't mean they're completely gone. Sometimes it's difficult to overcome our decisions, but if we can view the decision as a lesson in humility, we might be able to move on from there. The one thing we should not do is continue to live in the past, because to do so is demeaning to our life now.

When we continually berate ourselves for past mistakes, we disassociate ourselves from our higher purpose in life. We separate ourselves from our natural state of joy. If we're willing to stop looking regretfully at the past, value what we have now, and decide from here forth to act with gratitude in our hearts rather than regret, we'll be able to pick-up the pieces and carry on, and maybe teach others by example in the process. Regret wears you down and doesn't help you foster connections that will help you. You may find that you didn't even need a lot of those dominos. If you'll just allow yourself a little time, things will change for the better. And stop 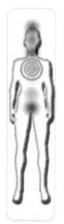 regretting past decisions; you'll make better decisions next time. Practice forgiveness and gratitude, and the dominos will begin to reset.

Seven of Swords

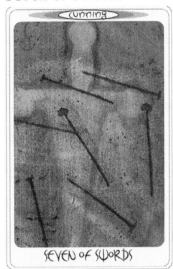

Keyword: Cunning
Chakra: Sacral, Orange

What you are building toward is doomed to failure if you take too many short-cuts. You are only deceiving yourself and denying yourself the just rewards you seek if you continue to use inferior thinking and means to get to your desired outcome. In White Light Tarot's Seven of Swords we see seven rusty nails that represent the meager tools that are being substituted for tools of truth and substance. In essence, the rusty nails represent deception and skilled use of cunning to manipulate a situation. When we kid ourselves about something being "good enough," or "okay" when we know in our hearts that it isn't, we are engaging in dishonesty, though being genuine and real all the time is easier said than done.

If the Seven of Swords comes up in a reading you need to ask yourself some tough questions. It's time for a little tough love, especially if you're avoiding the truth and not whole-heartedly behind what you're doing. You may need to figure out what you're running away from, and why you're avoiding confrontation, or you may need to figure out why you're exacerbating a problem by sneaking around the issue.

Whatever it is you are up against, face it head-on, be honest with yourself, and acknowledge that being shrewd or cunning might be part of the problem. If you're engaged in pulling the wool over someone's eyes, or hiding something from yourself, or simply deluding yourself by not admitting something that you know is true, progress can be difficult. That's the hardest part though, admitting that you've not been truthful, or that you've not been crystal clear in a situation. Once you allow yourself to see your role in the problem, then the solutions will come much more easily.

Think of a builder using the wrong grade of nail or un-galvanized nails for exterior work. Using regular nails or old nails from another job might do the trick for now and save the builder some time and effort, but in the long run, the job won't last, and eventually the builder will be exposed for his shabby technique. Put another way, the Seven of Swords is saying, do your duty, quit your whining and do what you must to "straighten up and fly right" and compete with honor. Admit it if you made a mistake. Face up to your responsibilities. Don't expect others to read your mind, you may have to tell them where you stand, but by doing so, you increase your self-respect, and probably their respect for you. It's okay to have a competitive nature, and a competitive edge, but if you've been coasting, don't shirk your responsibilities and expect to get away with it for long. If you're not up to the task, then drop out of the running and find a different way to accomplish your goals honorably. The Seven of Swords is a cautionary card, saying that you should not take advantage of the situation because it may well come back and bite you in the *arse*.

Reversed: Be careful whom you work with, they may not be as trustworthy as you think. If you think that you've been deceived, then you probably have. Subconscious motivations may come to the surface unexpectedly in an embarrassing moment. Recognize that these frailties are human, and everyone has them. Don't allow yourself to be victimized, but don't force yourself upon another either. Endeavor to work together as equals.

Six of Swords

SIX OF SWORDS

Keyword: Insight
Chakra: Brow, Indigo

The Six of Swords represents the direct insight that explodes in the mind when you "get it." When you finally understand some concept that was difficult for you, and you have an "ah-ha" moment - that is what the Six of Swords is about: the Eureka moment, the sudden insight, the moment when everything is obvious, and everything falls into place. But more than that, the Six of Swords is about enlightenment and acceptance.

The image of someone at a computer with lightening bolts is used to demonstrate the instantaneous connections that burst into existence when we "get" new concepts. At the same time these moments can lead to feeling overwhelmed and getting too much information too quickly. Both ways lead to inner expansion and understanding but one way is sudden and clear, and the other way is slow and painful.

In Herman Hess's story *Siddhartha*,[21] part of the Buddha's path towards enlightenment is helping mankind as a ferryman. As an old man, Siddhartha ferries people across the river, and the river and the rocks have taught him about life. He has learned that the flow is more powerful than stability, i.e., the river is more powerful than the rock. And by listening to a river's murmuring, he finds the peace of *OM* and personal transformation. The Six of Swords is a powerful card and one that isn't about sadness, unless the seeker refuses to accept that the path to enlightenment is different for everyone.

Buddha proclaimed the Four Noble Truths.
1. Life is sorrow.
2. Cause for sorrow is craving.

3. Removing the cause of craving will end sorrow.
4. The way that leads to the ending of sorrow is the noble Eight-Fold path.

At the end of his life Siddhartha tells his friend who has been seeking enlightenment that too much searching can preclude finding the truth, and that he at last had found his own enlightenment by listening to the river. Dogma or "...words and teachings may describe the truth but are not the Truth itself; being concepts, they trap you, since enlightenment means release from concepts." [22] Seek Karma and listen to your heart for your personal transformation and chant "OM" (ॐ).

Reversed: Don't go against the flow, you'll only tire yourself out. You can close your mind or open it – it's all up to you. Try to sit still and listen to what you really need to hear at this time. You may find you can ignite your facility for understanding more quickly if you will quit seeking and just allow it to happen gracefully in its right time.

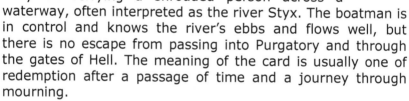

You're working too hard. Ease up and relax your grip a bit; you may find you know more than you thought you did in an instant.

The art for this card is a departure from the standard Rider-Waite. Some interpretations of the standard Six of Swords read this as a sorrowful card, and read a sinister aspect into journeying against one's will. The standard image is of a ferryman ferrying a shrouded person across a waterway, often interpreted as the river Styx. The boatman is in control and knows the river's ebbs and flows well, but there is no escape from passing into Purgatory and through the gates of Hell. The meaning of the card is usually one of redemption after a passage of time and a journey through mourning.

I would argue that the image of the ferryman could be interpreted as Siddhartha showing us the way to enlightenment if we would just remove our shroud and listen to the river. To support this, please note that the Tarot is generally thought to have travelled through India as it was developing and was dispersed by the Romany, a tribe that would have been familiar with Buddhist concepts. Buddhism applied to this card would be no farther a reach than Greek myth. In fact, I would argue the concepts of the Four Noble Truths are played out in the Rider-Waite card as much as the myth of the river Styx. I'm not sure that the concept of crossing the river is ever attributed to an image of the Buddha as a ferryman. At least I've never seen it discussed when looking at the Rider-Waite deck.

Five of Swords

FIVE OF SWORDS

Keyword: Shame
Chakra: Root, Red

The Five of Swords is about overcoming isolation and recognizing that your imprison- ment is of your own doing. When we experience isolation and hu- miliation, it is most likely because we are embarrassed by our past behavior. Psychological devastation has cut us to the quick, and it stings. Humiliation is a forced state of humility. Humility is the quality of being modest, respectful and having an unassuming nature. An un- assuming nature means being down-to-earth, able to connect to others lovingly and joy- fully, being sociable. When we get the Five of Swords, something has gone awry to make us feel ashamed. Maybe we've overstepped our boundaries, or made claims about how great we are that separated us from others emotionally. We sought approval a little too hard, and ended up alienated. We need to find a way to get back down to earth, apologize, if that's what it takes, or give in to the non-inclusiveness of the situation and walk away. Whatever is going on, as it stands now, it's a no- win situation. You may have bested your opponent, but the victory will feel hollow without compatriots to share it with. Find a way to reconnect with others who appreciate your efforts, but don't be arrogant about your abilities or it will lead to further isolation.

Reversed: Don't allow self-criticism to overtake your ability to see the situation clearly. Using your knowledge for gain rather than enlightenment or betterment of mankind leads to fatigue and de- fensive behavior. Share with others and you'll be able to overcome any social issue. You have nothing to be ashamed of if you are being who you really are.

Be true to yourself, if others can't accept you as you are, then you may need to move on. It is a painful situation perhaps, but one that will heal in time. As Eleanor Roosevelt so aptly put it, "No one can make you feel inferior without your consent." Using underhanded measures to outwit the opponent and win leaves one feeling a hollow victory.

Four of Swords

Keyword: Harmony
Chakra: Heart, Green

Alone but not lonely, the Four of Swords is bathed in the harmonious vibration of its own creation. A guitarist listens to the notes he struck fall together melodiously. Rather than actual swords, this image uses the sound vibration of a guitar chord as the swords. When we say "you struck a chord" we mean that something has resonated with us, that some feeling is sustained, and a type of stabilization is recorded in the fibers of our being. The musical imagery is not arbitrary; our lives are the interplay of tension and release that creates resolution in a final tune. The metaphor is apt, and the vocalization or vibratory representation of peace or discordance in a selected series of tones can be tracked through biofeedback, among other instruments, and can literally record our actual physiological responses to stimuli. Regardless of whether it may seem harmonious to your ears, the notes of your life will eventually fall together to create a symphony. Cooperation and sustaining stabilization are aspects of this card. See your life in harmony with what you want to achieve. You are a harmoniously vibrating being; remember that and you will continuously raise your vibration.

Reversed: Wait and listen when you get the Four of Swords reversed. It means you are feeling discordant and not in harmony with your surroundings. Maybe you need to be alone for a while. Sometimes it takes time to not feel lonely when we are alone. We need to adjust our vibration and learn to appreciate who we are, and if we are not happy with who we are then we need to work on changing that. You should be able to sit with yourself in peace and harmony. If you're having trouble doing that, then find someone with whom you feel safe and comfortable, but try to figure out why you need them to feel okay about yourself. Do they see you differently than you see yourself? Try to see yourself through their eyes. Keep the comforting image in your thoughts when you are alone. Eventually, you may want to call on your higher self, Source, or God, whatever you want to call it, to validate that you are okay alone.

Three of Swords

Keyword: Separation
Chakra: Brow, Indigo

The Three of Swords is about feeling dejected and separated from others: feeling rejected, alone, hurt, and not seeing beyond the pain. The expression "foiled again" springs to mind since three fencing foils are used instead of swords. The foils represent the three aspects of pain we often feel when we experience sorrow. We feel sorry for ourselves, we feel a loss of connection with others, and we often feel angry at life or God for our loss. When we experience sorrow or separation, we experience a depth of feeling we may not have known was possible to feel. It can hurt physically in our chest or heart, as well as emotionally, mentally and psychically.

But the pain is also a measure of the joy and comfort that we have lost. The psychic blades are piercing and wounding the mind, seemingly beyond repair, but whatever wrong has been done, it has ended. Look up, because it's over. Healing can begin, and the pain will pass. In the long silence of reflection we slowly find joy again. In the Three of Swords we see the sky is getting lighter and slowly dawn will burn away the hurt.

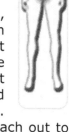

In our separation and disconnection from others, we will eventually reconnect with ourselves, which is the first step towards the healing process. First we need to reconnect with that quiet place inside where we are safe and comfortable. Once that takes place we can start to move on. We can find the strength to rise and leave the foils behind. Healing can take time, and it can be difficult to reach out to others. If that is too hard to do, then begin by opening yourself to receiving from others, and the pain of being alone will being to subside. Start by remembering that you are not alone; we are all connected.

Reversed: When something is too painful to deal with, we run away or find a way to bury or forget the hurt and anger. We try not to think about it, but in so doing we push our-selves farther away from acceptance and healing. When the Three of Swords is reversed, we may need to face some as-pect of our life head-on, one that has been causing us problems. If we continue to ignore the problem, life will even-tually throw us a curve ball and force us to deal with it a little too rapidly. If you want to live life to the fullest then you have to learn to accept the good with the bad and integrate problems into your life as a learning experience. Learning to love and to accept ourselves fully is part of why we are here.

Two of Swords

Keyword: Truce
Chakra: Throat, Light Blue

The Two of Swords is the reluctant beginning of cooperation. It marks a truce agreement to end hostilities, but a watchful and cautious end. In medieval Europe, from the mid-12th century to the mid-16th century, the 'longsword' and the 'bastard-sword' were the common blades of choice. The name 'bastard sword' comes from the fact that the weapon could be used as a one-handed or two-handed weapon. It didn't belong to either category so it was called a 'bastard.' The longsword was a bit narrower and tapered, and it was a cross between a dagger and a broadsword. The late medieval period in Europe still had use for a battlefield blade, but one that was light and maneuverable, so these were the blades of choice.

In the Two of Swords we see the longsword and bastard blade are both blades of compromise, hence the use of this iconography. They serve our meaning on several levels. One meaning takes into account the "difficult to sell ideas" represented by the broadsword combining with the "flurry of ideas that passes in and out of consciousness quickly" represented by the dagger. Finding an elegant solution to an impasse is represented by the peace lily in the center of the image. When getting this card, a leveling is taking place, a compromise is being agreed, an accord is in the offing, but be cautious, for these are two-edged blades that can still cut, and ideas are only as strong as the mind's ability to absorb and utilize them.

Reversed: The agreement is not to your liking and you resist it. If a compromise is not to be found, then you will have to fight. Are you willing to fight the forces surrounding you to get your way? Will it end in alienation if you win? What must you give up in order to achieve a compromise? Seeking a workaround isn't always a bad thing. When we allow other options to filter in, imagination is broadened and possibilities that we may not have recognized at first are visible. Don't underestimate the value of cooperation; it will create allies.

Ace of Swords

Keyword: Exact
Chakra: Solar Plexus, Yellow

This card represents pinpoint accuracy. When you get the Ace of Swords, you've hit the proverbial nail on the head. This card is like the big bang at the beginning of time. From one single point in time and space, the universe unfolds and expands outward. This is the start of something big. You're in the right place at the right time so savor the moment. If you don't act quickly, you may miss your chance, so stay alert and pay attention to synchronicity. "Carpe diem." You are no longer disabled by doubt, confusion or indecision. Whatever it is that you've had in mind to do, don't delay, do it now; there is no better time than the present. You have aligned your thoughts and feelings, so go for it. Deciding is half the battle. Once you've decided and truly committed yourself to a decision, don't second guess yourself, take action and watch as things fall into place. When you get the Ace of Swords, it is an indication that you should take immediate action to put your dreams into play.

Reversed: You are resisting making the decision and if you continue to resist, a decision will be made for you, and it may not be the one you would have chosen. Be careful that you don't miss an opportunity. Admittedly, not all opportunities need to be taken, but sometimes we have to meet our fears head-on and take the plunge. Fear can freeze us into a standstill where we don't grow, and we begin to wither and die. Don't let others decide for you, you know what is best for you. Even if you make the "wrong" choice, you will learn from your mistakes. Do what you think is best for you.

THE WANDS

Historically in the Tarot, the Wands have represented the peasant or heathen class, meaning people who live in the heath and work the land. The wand or staff is a tool that is usually made of wood and is used to harness momentum. Wands channel muscle as a plow, speed as a walking stick, or psychic force acting as a focal point for wielding life energy.

The wand is a conduit between energy transmutations. Trees grow up from the land, their energy bringing together earth (roots), air (branches) and water (blood), yet the tree is combustible by nature. Wands harnessed become the keeper of flame which translates into emotional passion, intellectual examination, and spiritual awe.

The King of Wands

KING of WANDS

Keyword: Passion
Chakra: Root, Red

The King of Wands is in a never-ending wrestling match with the royal stag. The battle is to tame the passions and harness or control the energy released through the Kundalini. In many traditions, the stag is a symbol of strength and purity of the soul. It is also a symbol of male virility. The stag is linked with the "tree of life" or immortality and to the "king of kings" or Jesus. However, the stag is an even more complex symbol because in addition to virility, power and purity, it also represents timidity and innocence. So when you get this card, you need to consider the context in which it is being seen.

In many European traditions the stag is the ultimate symbol of sexual ardor, prudence, healing, poetry and song. Shakespeare made puns on the word 'hart' and 'heart' in his play, *Twelfth Night*, and there are plenty of myths that involve men changing into stags. For example, the Celtic god Cernunnos would change into a stag when he was in the forest, and in Greek myth, Artemis turned Actaeon into a stag because he glimpsed her bathing. Heracles' third task was to capture the stag with golden antlers. Though Heracles himself didn't change into a stag, he did recapture his honor as predicted by the Delphic Oracle by completing this task and eleven others which are known as "The Twelve Labors of Hercules." In Cambodian literature the stag was the herald of fire.

To sum it up, let's look at a quote found in the Hermetic tract *The Book of Lambspring*. "...the deer desires no other name than that of soul...he that knows how to tame and master... may justly be called Master."[23]

So the majesty of the stag that is part of the King of Wands is part of his power and allure. The King of Wands is a very charismatic and charming person. He's that guy with a lot of sex appeal for both sexes, regardless of their orientation. He has animal magnetism and pheromones that keep him in the spotlight, even if he doesn't want to be there. He probably uses "his powers" to good advantage. Often he'll be overly promiscuous, but he may be the other extreme and harbor his pent-up energy for other purposes. If he understands his power and can tame it, then there's no stopping him.

Reversed: Kundalini energy, if released prematurely, can be very scary and painful. Emotional or life-threatening situations can manifest a rise in Kundalini energy without the person understanding what's happening to him or her. The body quakes or vibrates involuntarily, and the Kundalini reenergizes or turns-on the repressed emotional (psychosomatic) areas of the mind. If left unchecked, the rising energy forces old trauma to manifest in dreams, and as past life memories. In most people the complete rise of "serpent power" is blocked because of our psycho-social upbringing. Hatha yoga has asanas that are designed to engage and release it in a more controlled manner, and meditation and yoga practice can help tame the Kundalini if released too quickly. When the Kundalini awakens involuntarily, it can feel unrelenting. In most instances, it burns away and heals old wounds, but the passions may be ignited as it happens. If you get the King of Wands reversed, you're probably in for a bumpy emotional ride. The passions will be aflame as the karma is clearing. The process often is very intense, and you will probably feel exhausted, but by clearing away old emotional baggage, you'll make room for new experiences in life. It won't be easy, but once you get through this, you'll never have to do it again.

The Queen of Wands

QUEEN of WANDS

Keyword: Generous
Chakra: Heart, Green

The Queen of Wands, aided by her stave, quickly climbs to the highest point on the mountaintop. Her stride is long and confident. She likes stories, and has a cadre of them. When she tells one, she doesn't hold back. She is opinionated, a revolutionary at the core, so her words can seem scorching at first, but her aim is not to envelope you but to include you, she is only using what you offer as fuel for the fire. She is hardy and laughs easily, knowing that there is nothing to worry about.

She is confident in her abilities, and isn't really judgmental. She'll tease you and fully expects to be teased; it keeps her humble and real. Don't overreact to her fiery nature. She only wants to be your friend.

Burning the candle at both ends is not unusual for her. In fact, it's how she best thrives. Like the flame of an open fire, she is warm and welcoming, but don't sit too close or you risk getting scorched. Quick-witted and physically adept, she is as graceful and agile in the boardroom as she is on a ski slope or roller blades. She's a very well-rounded and adventurous person, but she's hard to keep up with.

This card indicates a positive turn of events, either someone you know or you yourself should be beaming with confidence. You are attracting the right people and the right situations to you. The Queen of Wands says not to worry about a thing, just maintain the effortless enthusiasm that has propelled you this far and you'll find yourself on the top of the mountain in no time.

Reversed: When you get the Queen of Wands reversed, it probably means you're acting like a brat. This fiery lady won't back down, and coercion isn't pretty. Whatever is going on, even if you're right, you can't win by being a bully. Eagerness to jump headlong into something isn't everyone's cup of tea. Your teasing may have turned into malicious mockery. If you've crossed the line, apologize. Being annoyed won't get things done any quicker. You may need to find another strategy to get where you want to go.

The Knight of Wands

Keyword: Alchemical
Chakra: Sacral, Orange

The Knight of Wands is a very energetic young man who possesses what the Egyptians term "intelligence of the heart." When rational thought and intuitive feeling are joined, it is called the "conjunction of the Overself' in alchemy. Simply put, the Overself is the ability to maintain presence of mind; it is the ability to maintain the state of awareness or inner knowing that we are all connected and one. It is when our personality gives way to our higher self. Once this state is attained it allows us to see the big picture for the greater good all the time. This state of mind is something that must be practiced, however. As the joining of the two aspects of both male and female elements becomes easier for the Knight of Wands to maintain, he creates distance from judgmental or emotional behavior no matter what happens, and he remains calm.

Practice maintaining your presence of mind no matter what emotions well up in you. When you come across inconsiderate or spiteful behavior in others, remind yourself that this is a reflection of something within yourself. All problems, every miscommunication, every annoying person, every confusing situation is an opportunity to practice the development of the Overself. You can tell you are maintaining this state when you laugh at stupid things that used to make you angry. When you keep your cool and you don't lash out at someone's insensitivity towards you, you are maintaining the Overself. This card indicates growth in the ability to maintain the enlightened understanding that we are all connected. The conjunction of the male and female aspects of self manifest in the sacral chakra, so getting this card indicates the beginning of personal transformation and the empowerment of your true consciousness.

This card indicates a slow release of Kundalini power. It indicates a quick resolution to any worries you've had. This maintained conscious connection to the divine self is the true domain of the Knight of Wands, and it results in lightning-fast thought. Thoughts are transmuted into reality effortlessly through the use of his stave. The Knight of Wands is in principle a magician in training, the alchemist of Iran's 14th century.

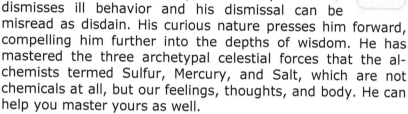

The Knight of Wands is quick tempered and can come off as arrogant in an argument. This is because he knows the truth of our existence, and that there is no cause for worry, so when pressed he dismisses ill behavior and his dismissal can be misread as disdain. His curious nature presses him forward, compelling him further into the depths of wisdom. He has mastered the three archetypal celestial forces that the alchemists termed Sulfur, Mercury, and Salt, which are not chemicals at all, but our feelings, thoughts, and body. He can help you master yours as well.

Reversed: Like King Philip IV of France, indebted to the Knights Templar and purposefully burning them at the stake to get out of repaying his debt, someone or some aspect of yourself is trying to undermine your power. Although the date doesn't actually correspond to Friday the 13th, the arrest of the Knights Templar on October 13, 1307 has become associated with the unluckiness of Friday the 13th. You're walking around with a little black cloud over your head, and you'll lose your energy if you continue doing what you're doing, or associating with someone that isn't honoring you.

The Knights Templar controlled great wealth and power throughout Europe and the Middle East. This monastic order was the first international organization, and lasted almost 400 years. The Knights Templar were brought down by a new papal regime and economic strain. The story of the demise of the Knights Templar, or their fall from grace indicates that you're not recognizing your indebtedness to your higher self.

You are on your way to getting what you desire out of life. Recognize that you have a controlling interest in what happens and undertake to give thanks for your Overself, making sure that you stay connected to the greater white light web of life.

Page of Wands

PAGE OF WANDS

Keyword: Ambition
Chakra: Solar Plexus, Yellow

Behind dark eyes is an all-consuming flame. The Page of Wands has only just picked up the torch. He is very talented and ambitious, and he wants to test his new-found confidence. With so many options at his disposal, it will be difficult to choose only one area to channel his energy into, but that is his challenge. Igniting the passions is easy for the Page of Wands, but deciding the best way to direct all of that creative energy can be problematic. If he decides to help others, his passion will generate opportunities for him, but at the other extreme, if he acts selfishly, he may find that he gets burned by those around him. He is just learning to wield the fire of his will and direct its flow into something that he is passionate about. He has a lot to learn, and he has a difficult time remembering humility. Once he has decided how he will pursue his ambitions, all the rest will fall into place for good or ill.

One of his lessons is learning to wait and receive. His tendency is to force his will to the exclusion of everything else. If he does this continually, he will burn out.

When you get the Page of Wands you will probably experience sudden bursts of emotion and frenetic behavior. The Page of Wands means there are a number of different options available. The best option is to move forward with one focal point in mind, but the task is deciding where to place that forceful energetic touch.

Reversed: Tantrums, fits of laughter, or angry outbursts are indicated when the Page of Wands is reversed. Growing pains can happen physically, emotionally, psychically or spiritually. You are having growing pains. The more you are able to relax and go with the flow, the easier it will be to integrate your new-found power. Ambition is another way of saying "remember your dreams." Keep your dreams in the forefront of your mind, and when you experience tantrums, good or bad, psychic or physical, know that changes are taking place and that growth is assured.

Ten of Wands

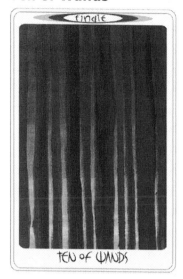

TEN of WANDS

Keyword: Finale
Chakra: Root, Red

The Ten of Wands is the sigh at the end of the day, the letting go of any worry or desired outcome and appreciating what is and what we have. The setting sun through the trees reminds us that in the end, it is not so much what we accomplished, but how we got there that counts. The trees represent not only growth, triumph, and accumulation, but depending on the circumstance, they conversely represent any blocks we have experienced in reaching our goals. We must work with all of the elements in tandem to see good results. When we are rooted in one way of thinking, we diminish our ability to grow. We run the risk of become stunted, unwilling to compromise, and experiencing difficulty in finding nourishment. If we stay open, allowing the breeze to sway us, the earth, water and light to nurture us then we will continue to mature, become stronger and more able to expand and share our resources with others to make a stronger natural system.

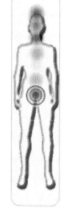

Trees keep the soil in place and give us life-enhancing oxygen, shade and food. Without them the earth would be overexposed. We need others to enhance our appreciation of what we experience. When we can let go of our desires and discriminate between what is real and unreal, what are true accomplishments versus simple activities, we will know through intense contemplation that we are part of a large united system, the ultimate mind if you will, and effortlessly, we will know how to continually enhance this natural system.

Reversed: If our goal is to shine like the sun, full of light, warmth and color, then we must break through the cycle of *samsara* (ongoing cycle of birth, death, and rebirth) to the light from within. You have achieved much, but always remember your divinity and be thankful.

Nine of Wands

NINE of WANDS

Keyword: Zenith
Chakra: Crown, Violet

The Nine of Wands represents a rest period in your life because you have accomplished what you set out to do. When you get this card, you should draw your community together to help you celebrate your achievement. Recognize your skill and welcome the rest and relaxation. You deserve to use the reset button on occasion, use it wisely. Through awakened Kundalini you are experiencing the height of ex-pectorations. Sometimes Kundalini is awakened violently. Hiroshima and Nagasaki were decimated in WWII, but out of the horror there emerged new heights in architecture. Kenzo Tange's building style has influenced the world, and it has paved the way for new innovations in Japanese art and architecture. The Nine of Wands represents the ultimate achievement of man overcoming all obstacles and creating a more robust future.

In White Light Tarot the Nine of Wands shows streaks of light against the mirrored glass of a modern building's windows. The idea is the expression of human innovation, whether found in architecture, a heart valve, language, God, cloning, a fast engine, the international space station, or nano-technology, whatever your notion of the pinnacle of achievement of man, this is it. You have achieved your highest point. Celebrate.

Reversed: You feel you've not lived up to your potential in some way. If you continue to worry about what you neglected to do, you'll only exacerbate the problem. Diversion isn't always bad, and sometimes it is necessary to find the next development along the path to the ultimate achievement. Diversity is from the same root as diversion, so don't worry about how it will all come together in the end. Though the end may not be in sight at the moment, eventually things will come together. We are always building upon our skills in some way if we are actively participating in the creation process. Don't sit on the couch and stew in front of the TV. Go out and find something that interests you and dig in, don't worry about the consequences of your actions unless it might hurt someone or yourself. If that's the case, then correct your misdeeds, but otherwise, find new and interesting ways to reach your own potential.

Eight of Wands

EIGHT OF WANDS

Keyword: Emanate
Chakra: Throat, Light-Blue

In the Eight of Wands we see a temple based on the one at Ephesus. In this image, the temple's pillars are eight actual wands reaching up towards the heavens. Stately and stable, the pillars course with energy. The fires are lit around them to burn away any fear and ineffectualness and to energize our thoughts into actions.

The temple at Ephesus was dedicated to Artemis and became one of the "Seven Wonders of the Ancient World." Artemis was worshipped as a fertility goddess, but she is also a deity dedicated to purity. Twin to Apollo, she is a huntress with bow and arrow, able to aim high and spot on. When you get the Eight of Wands, take your time, do not speak too soon and think before you act. The fires of ritual burn bright under a starry sky.

The communion of the elements of fire and air create the environment where you can rededicate yourself to whatever task is yours to do. Bring spirit and flesh together into one magnificent being. Burn away any doubt, and emanate your true self, your hopes and desires for yourself, for your community, for mankind and the planet. Communicate your highest goals for the good of all, and give thanks right now. Sacrifice to the gods, by pouring a bit of wine, mead, beer, or plain clear water in honor of them. They appreciate your efforts, and will assist you in moving forward. Release your energy to heaven, and allow your energy to rise like smoke from the fire.

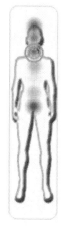

129

Reversed: You may have missed your chance this time around, but opportunities come and go. If you get the Eight of Wands reversed, don't worry about it too much; not every opportunity is for the taking, but you sort of missed the boat on this one. You'll need to raise your energy back up, as you've lost the flow for now. If it is something that you need to do, then the situation will arise again. Only next time you'll recognize it and be prepared to act. Carpe Diem because the only time we have is the present moment.

Seven of Wands

SEVEN OF WANDS

Keyword: Diversity
Chakra :Sacral, Orange

In the seventh circle of Dante's *Inferno*, Virgil leads Dante into the suicide forest. It is a sad forest, full of wailing, loss and unmet desires.

From The Purgatorio Canto XIII:

"The Spirit explained how suicides came to be sad trees: Minos sent them to the seventh circle as seeds, to sprout where they fell. After the last judgment they would bring their bodies down, but would not inhabit them, since as suicides they had no right to take them again: instead they would hang their bodies on their trees."

The imagery of Dante's suicide forest is used to demonstrate the despair that surrounds you: In the Seven of Wands a young pregnant woman full of life and hope walks alone through a forest of sad faces. Her responsibilities feel heavier as she walks through this forest of unsupportive, jeering and self-absorbed connections. Alone, she must learn to trust herself, develop her character and pay no mind to the naysayers. It is easy to lose hope when you are surrounded by negativity. Don't be a "sad sack" hanging from a tree of despair.

We are all pregnant with hope and possibility which we can grow. We develop character by calling upon our internal supports when faced with adversity, hostility and feeling alone. Do not give up, the Seven of Wands is saying, for within you is the seed of possibility, renewal and growth. Keep after your dreams; you will get through this forest of negativity. If you are brave you will succeed. Do not let your guard down, but be brave and press onward!

Reversed: You may feel emotionally lost, or you may have let your guard down a little too far. Sometimes we have to decide for ourselves who has our best interests at heart. We need to give ourselves a little sound advice. Unsolicited advice is often given by people needing advice, and the advice they offer is about their own needs and requirements for peace of mind. This is not to say you shouldn't share your feelings or your problems with others, but to always take advice with a grain of salt. Think for yourself and don't simply do a thing because you were advised to do so and it was touted as "good advice."

Six of Wands

SIX OF WANDS

Keyword: Inward
Chakra: Brow, Indigo

A figure is seated on the stone in the forest. His form is taken from Auguste Rodin's sculpture *The Thinker*. In 1880, Rodin aimed to depict Dante at the gates of hell in the traditional heroic statuary style, like Michelangelo's *David*. *The Poet,* as Rodin called his piece, became *The Thinker* by the time it was finished in 1902. The seated figure has come to represent higher learning, philosophy, and man's internal struggle - an icon of intellectual activity. In the Six of Wands, our thinker sits on a rock in a grove of birch trees. He is journeying inward, yet psychically radiating outwardly his innermost energy. His presence penetrates through the forest's floor, helping to ground him. The energy recycles back to him, wrapping him in peace, tranquility, depth and gratitude. This energy soothes his worry and allows him to radiate his innermost self outward without fear. His thoughts and breaths fall into sync with mother earth's, the two are one and reverberate and pulse with nurturing energy. His victory is in allowing this natural communion and knowing he is capable of serenity. The achievement that is celebrated externally is often hollow; those that we celebrate internally are much more lasting. Connect with your breath, connect with the earth. You have worked hard, thought hard, loved hard and what you have done has paid off internally if not externally. Breathe to clear your worries, breathe to renew your connection.

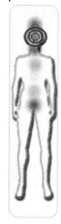

Reversed: You may be trying too hard when you get the Six of Wands reversed. Finding new connections isn't as hard as you think. Engage and enlarge your sphere of influence simply by deciding to allow connections to appear. Learning something new takes concentration, but actually understanding it can take a lifetime. There are many different aspects to connections and learning. Passion plays a role in our abilities, so does inspiration. So use your passions to inspire. Remembering that we are much more than we appear to be can help us to maintain our optimism. The rods or wands are about passion and development of spiritual connection. Although cliché, an optimistic attitude will more often than not lead to some sort of victory, and even if that victory doesn't receive external acknowledgement it will probably lead to connections you can't even imagine. So don't get hung up on why things are like they are; just do your best and stay optimistic. The connections will come as you learn. Be open.

Five of Wands

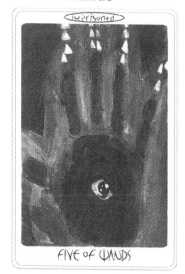

FIVE OF WANDS

Keyword: Imprisoned
Chakra: Solar Plexus, Yellow

This is a very complex symbol. Problems must be solved with skill, and belief in one's abilities is at issue. The feeling that this card represents is an inability to cope with what lies in front of you. Ultimately, in combining the spiral, eye and red hand into one symbol, what we have is knowledge imprisoned in flesh. The fingers and thumb are the five wands. Wands direct energy from the spark of imagination through to manifestation. In this painting, the color red represents the physical manifestation of our bodies, and the spiral represents our own ability to heal. The eye is our true inner knowing which shows us that we must first recognize our abilities as real and meaningful in order to manifest our destiny. Our imprisonment is only in our minds, but our minds are very powerful.

Recognize your mind's role in whatever holds you back. Breaking through your limitations is the task to be solved. This is a very powerful symbol to meditate on, as it strikes not only the root chakra and psychic chakra but also the solar plexus. This image could help banish fear and oppression and help you connect to your internal bodhisattva.

The hand with a wheel, eye or spiral in the palm is a very old and pan-cultural symbol. In India the 'Ahimsa' symbol (wheel in the palm) is used by the Jains to communicate the idea that through concentration one can halt the wheel of re-incarnation by practicing "non-injury," which is the literal meaning of *ahimsa*. The meaning of the eye in the palm varies a little culturally, but almost always the idea includes combining omnipotence (all powerful) and omniscience (all knowing). The symbol is seen in most bodhisattva's hands like Buddha, White Tara and Quan Yin, where it means "the merciful (person) acts with full knowing and seeing."

Another version found in the Middle East uses a blue eye in the center of the palm and is called the Hamsa amulet. It is used for protection to ward off the evil eye, and is known as "God's Protective Hand." Interestingly, perhaps because of genetic rarity in that part of the world, Turkey and Greece hold that the "evil eye" is blue, so the 'Hamsa' is made by placing a translucent blue glass eye in the center of the palm, and it is used to ward off the evil eye.

In Tibet, the word changes a little and is pronounced *Humsa*. Rather than warding off the evil eye, in Tibet the symbol banishes fear and oppression. It is also known as the "All-seeing eye of Mercy," which is in keeping with the bodhisattva's meaning of the "Ahimsa." The eye in the palm is also known as the Egyptian eye of Maat, again a symbol for protection, and in some Native American cultures the eye in the hand is for protection as well. Spirals in hands are found in the Americas as far south as Peru and as far North as Canada, and in some parts of Europe. The spiral in the hand is a symbol for the healing hand, and is a symbol used in Reiki.

Reversed: Put into practice what you know is true. You can banish fear and oppression. Give yourself permission to use your hands creatively. You can make a commitment to learn to love better, more, and without judgment and while you do that you can also observe and explore love as a power that is flowing through you. Exercise your creative abilities; create something. We are more than we appear to be; your hands are gateways to Reiki energy. Harness that healing for a better world. Some studies in Japan have found that we radiate light biochemically, and our hands and fingernails emit the most particles. Use your hands wisely, and value the human characteristics that we can express with our hands.

Four of Wands

FOUR OF WANDS

Keyword: Psychic Force
Chakra: Brow, Indigo

The stability of the four pillars allows you to call in your forces and build anew. It is time for you to harvest the stored energy. Just like a piece of fruit is the accumulation of the stored energy that started as a seed, you have within you something that is ready for harvest. "Energetically," now is the time to call in your creative abilities and force them to a focal point.

A departure from the usual image of fruit trees heavy with fruit, in the White Light Tarot interpretation the Four of Wands is an image of a human figure atop the four pillars of thought, or the foundation of knowledge. The figure is actively calling in the four winds, and the energy is amassing in and around the human form who is about to release an immense psychic blast. Note that in this card the human figure is calling in his forces; he has yet to focus them. The energy is immense and, when he is ready, he will have amassed a great wealth of energy. How he harvests that energy has yet to be determined.

Other 'four pillars' symbols include the concept of destiny in Chinese astrology and Feng Shui. Our destiny is made of the four parts of Fate, marked by the year, month, hour and minutes of our birth. In the Green Party the four pillars are ecological wisdom, social justice, grassroots democracy, and nonviolence. For the Moldova nation the four pillars are a declaration of independence as a small separatist nation in Eastern Europe.

All of these uses of the four pillars have one thing in common: they have declared their destiny by using the four pillars to create a stable support for their beliefs. Harness your energy in a stable environment and you'll see the fruits of your labor. It is time for you to channel your abilities, appetites, and creativity into a powerful force. The pillars are the four wands, which offer the foundation for clarity and letting go of limitation. This card is about freedom and creation.

Your true destiny is to declare yourself master of your own fate. But if it helps you clear away the clutter, then go ahead and call upon the mythical source called the *Fates* and seek their aid in finding your destiny. The Fates have many names: they are the *Moirae* in Greek mythology or the *Parcae* in Roman mythology. In Norse mythology, Fate is known as the *Norns*, and an ancient version of Fate from northwestern Europe is known as the *Matres*. You must stabilize your environment, stabilize your beliefs, stabilize your body and then let go of any limitations by focusing your energies on creating your true destiny with an immense psychic blast. Think of thoughts as in-vitro actions. Think clearly, and wisely.

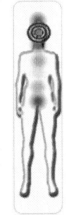

Reversed: You lose power every time you focus on the problem. This is not to say that you shouldn't question authority or find a better way to do something, but always stay focused on the solution. Focus on what you think you really want, right now. That may change, and that's okay, but stay focused on what you want, not on what you don't want. The limitations that you let go of allow you to create a larger psychic force or area of what you do want. This is as potent as your instinctual drives, because it is one of them. The chemicals in our brains are what create our destiny as much as anything else, so endeavor to create an environment that helps you harness your energy in a way that will help you harvest your highest goals and ideals. Focus on what you want, and call the energy to you.

Three of Wands

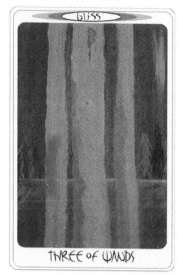

THREE of WANDS

Keyword: Bliss
Chakra: Heart, Green

The old master Joseph Campbell said, "Follow your bliss."[24] The bind rune for joy and growth is carved on the middle tree in White Light Tarot's Three of Wands. Following your bliss means continually growing, expanding, and purposefully finding ways of expressing joy and appreciation. When you get the Three of Wands you need to do the thing that is effortless and that makes you feel good. Find your bliss and follow it; that's the dictate of this card. For some people this card means going out and exploring options; they may not quite know what they're good at. They need to take some chances to find it, or maybe exploring options is their bliss. For others this card means to slow down, to go ahead and coast along, to enjoy life, to quit striving so much, to realize that you're fine as you are.

When you do what makes you feel useful, effective and happy as often as you can, you are actively following your bliss. The Three of Wands is also about virtue, but being virtuous isn't hard. The virtuous are just people who practice being good at what they're good at and at what they like doing. Don't get hung up on the Christian spin of virtue and vice. Hopefully, what you're good at has a benefit for the greater populace. In the greater sense of the word, to be virtuous is to be at peace, joyfully doing what you're good at. "Taken in its widest sense virtue refers to excellence, just as vice, its contrary, denotes the absence of such. In its strictest meaning, however, as used by moral philosophers and theologians, virtue is an operative habit essentially good, as distinguished from vice, an operative habit essentially evil."[25]

When you get this card, endeavor to be like trees, growing, strong, resilient, pliant, giving, and effortlessly joyful. But we are also here to express emotion and experience all of its complexity, so it's okay to feel bad, or angry, or confused. But joy is our natural state, so find ways to enhance that state in your life. To celebrate getting the Three of Wands, maybe go out and give a tree a hug; okay, maybe just water a tree. However you decide to celebrate, you are celebrating the idea of effortlessly growing into who you are best at being.

We are always in a state of becoming. Know that simply by being you, by being here, you are an asset to the world. Feel the bliss of being an asset to the world without worry. Stand tall with virtue, without arrogance. Be who you really are without hubris, without feigned humility. You are a dynamic, graceful being, so stay passionate about what you're good at. Stay focused and self-motivated to do what you are best at. Lead or follow – it doesn't matter. What matters is that you feel good about doing a good job at what you're doing. When you are joyful and focused, you accommodate with ease. Following your bliss doesn't give you permission to degenerate into your addictions, it means to live your life joyfully. Find that thing that when you're involved in it, you lose sight of time. Following our bliss is effortlessly doing what needs to be done.

Reversed: You may be having trouble finding joy in your life. If you are feeling stunted in some area or malnourished in some way, find a way to supplement your emotional life to get back your spark and passion. When you get the Three of Wands reversed, the cards are saying you might not be experiencing full-fledged depression, but feeling uneasy or sad. This isn't easy to live with, so find small ways to make yourself feel better so that you recognize yourself again. If you don't know what makes you happy, don't sink into food, alcohol or drugs as an escape. Find something that is productive that will help you connect with others. Inspirational movies and books, book clubs or a walk in the park where you can pat a few dogs might help you feel better when you're out of sorts. Do things that you enjoy doing. This card is telling you to take action, to add pleasure and passion into your life.

Two of Wands

Keyword: Steady
Chakra: Throat, Light-Blue

Mounting courage to take on a task, slow and steady, you are in control of your actions, and you may have some control over others. Use it wisely. A kind yet stern nature is indicated when you get the Two of Wands. In this image, the rising sun beats down on two standing staves in a lake, perhaps the last remnants of a standing stones worship ring. The energetics represented is subtle yet powerful, as the Two of Wands examines the internal sources of passion and drive. The message is one of steadfastness, clarity and dynamism. Although the standing stones seem unmoving, over millennia they move as does the earth around them. Sun, water, rock and sky combine to make this place energetically fluid and dynamic, creating a sacred space. You have managed to create that sacred space within yourself. Drink in the image of the stones rising from the water into a burning sky. Experience the ability to "steady on" in any situation. Burn through any issues that you feel are holding you back to get to the solid solution underneath. Communicate your fluidity and solid commitment along with your burning desire to see whatever you need to through to the end, but remember to breathe and keep space within to renew and balance your energies wisely.

Reversed: You know what needs doing, and unlike some people, you actually have the means to see your ideas through. Whatever it is that is holding you back, you can face it, and you can find a way to master it, or find a way around it. Master your insecurities and fears by concentrating on improving

142

your skills patiently. Keep the passions in balance, and keep clearing away resistance.

Ace of Wands

Keyword: Furnace
Chakra: Root, Red

Focus your mind and stay excited about the task at hand. The Ace of Wands card means the beginning of enterprise and adventure, the start of releasing power, energy and passion, or the inkling of intuition. The power of the Ace of Wands largely is enthusiasm and feeling compelled to take action. When you get this card it is a signal that the spark of spirit necessary for the rise of Kundalini energy is taking place.

Kundalini is Sanskrit for 'coiled up.' Tantric yoga uses the term to describe energy stored at the base of the spine in a coil of subtle chakra energies. In English it is sometimes called 'serpent power.' To engage this subtle energy, yogis use postures or breathing techniques.

Sometimes being excited or eager can also cause this subtle energy to rise up through the Sushumna (center spinal energy conduit) from the root chakra to the crown and back again. While at the same time the subtle energies swirl and combine through the Ida (left feminine channel) and Pingala (right male channel) in a rush to escape through the crown. This is the opening of the chakra energy system. Control is necessary to enhance the opening of the subtle energies and to use them, so you might want to practice Pranayama breathing techniques. It is essentially yogic breathing. Breathing slowly with full inhalations and exhalations in three parts allows us to slow the release of Kundalini and control the energy. These techniques are part of pranic healing.

The Wands are the most mutable of the suits, hence the most adaptable, and the most prone to quick evolution and revolution. When you get the Ace of Wands you are demonstrating passion about some aspect of your life, and you are in a position to experience some kind of ramped-up change that will come on suddenly. Remain passionate, but temper it with sound judgment because the Wands will let you burn the candle at both ends, if you don't watch out, and you'll burn out quickly. The Wands are the phallic equivalent of the Empress' womb-like warmth. Celebration, creativity, and ambition forge together in the fiery furnace that holds the essence of the Wands. Celebrate your ideals passionately.

Reversed: If you keep up this pace, you'll burn out. Sometimes you need to let the fire burn down to coals. Let the flames die down, listen to the charcoal hiss and pop, watch the subtle flicker of the red coals. Coals are actually hotter than flames, and they work much better for toasting marshmallows. Marshmallows in flames simply burn up, but marshmallows over coals roast to a golden brown. Don't be in such a rush; you have all the energy you need to do what-ever it is you want to do, but you should allow for it to happen gradually. Patience.

5

THE CUPS

The two essential aspects of the suit of cups are those of a vessel of plenty, like the Norse drinking horn that never empties, and the draught of immortality, like in the story of the Holy Grail. Knot work is found in Celtic illumination art, and in the work of Leonardo da Vinci and Albrecht Dürer. It remains an artistic vision for expressing emotional enlightenment.

The King of Cups

Keyword: Serenity
Chakra: Heart, Green
The King of Cups is someone kind, gentle and responsible. It is likely he is connected with a world-scale political, religious, or medical organization, and he is a leader in his field. He is caring and he feels deeply. The king stands impressively unadorned, naked, revealing his vulnerability and displaying himself so openly, honestly and unabashedly that he is also displaying his strength. You needn't look away in shame; there is nothing to fear or be ashamed about. He radiates great love and compassion. Untie the knots in your emotional consciousness and allow the vibration of the lapping waters to spill over, soothing your mind and energy. The Celtic knot work on the Loving Cup is a symbol of completion and restoration. The King of Cups can offer you the grail which will heal your soul. Share the Loving Cup, if need be allow him to help you restore your inner peace. When you get this card, know that you are or will soon be restored to your loving nature.

Reversed: There are many stories about a king's healing abilities and his psychic connection with the land he rules. These parables make use of cyclic shortcomings: a task being almost complete then tragically falling short of its goal only to find redemption from an overlooked humble source.

The medieval Welsh Mabinogion tells the story of Bran the Blessed and the healing caldron; T.S. Eliot's poem *The Wasteland* is a post World War I look at desolation and redemption, and Malory's *Le Morte d'Arthur* tells the story of the Grail.

In the Fisher-King and the Grail, the king's terrible wound will not heal, and during the day, the king seeks solace in fishing, but his country is a wasteland, and it cannot support his people. The land is a reflection of the king's state – he is a waste, and so the land suffers as a wasteland. The Knight Percival finds the simple solution is to ask "what ails the king" after years of travail. When Percival truly follows his heart, he restores the grail and health to the king and his land.

The point is, just as the knight Percival must ask before it is too late, you too must ask your own King of Cups what ails him. Once broached, he will give forth without hesitation, but to approach him takes courage. You can heal your own internal Fisher-King and restore health to your inner landscape by forgiving yourself for your own shortcomings. Once we understand this and accept our shortcomings as being human, the King of Cups will invite us to drink the "milk of human kindness" and recognize our own reflection as that of kindred divinity. The serenity we seek is in our hearts. Let the mind relax, let the spirit become calm, let the emotional waters restore the garden of the King of Cups, and let us humbly watch the garden flourish.

The Queen of Cups

QUEEN of CUPS

Keyword: Raising Energy
Chakra: Crown, Violet

The Queen of Cups draws energy up and out from the silver cup at her feet. The fish on her right side are an offering for the physical manifestation of what she calls forth from the watery depths of emotion. Manifestation occurs "upon the face of the waters" and the queen draws forth what appears most important to her in the reflecting waters.

The offering of fish is significant: it is as if she were offering herself. The fish is an ancient and rich symbol. Because of the vast number of eggs fish lay when they spawn, fish are associated with prosperity, longevity, fertility and success. In Chinese symbolism to dream of eating carp is considered lucky, and to give a carp as a gift at the beginning of a venture ensures success. In some sea-faring cultures, a goddess was called "the chief of the fishes" – this is also the title given to the female dolphin.

The Greek word for fish (*ichthus*) became an ideogram for the Eucharist, and the fish became a symbol of faith for early Christians. As a sign of their devotion they were bound by the cup and the fish. Leviticus excluded fish as a sacrificial animal and they became a symbol of rebirth, faith in Christ, and Christ himself.

Like Christ, Vishnu's symbol is a fish, too. Vishnu became a fish to save Manu (father of the human race). This allowed him to bring forth the Vedas, which are the Hindi books of sacred knowledge. As fish, both Christ and Vishnu guide their respective arks to safety and feed the masses. Yoga was taught to man by a fish, and in yoga the fish is known as a symbol for wisdom. The fish, as a yoga pose, opens our communication chakra. Our Queen of Cups uses fish as a sacrifice because she is ascribing the fish with all the attributes of the higher mind's descent into emotional waters. She is telling you not to lose your head; use your emotional power to manifest your interests. Cast flower petals on a body of water and watch as the eddies and ripples take them out to sea, and know that this is the intersection of the subconscious and reality.

This woman can get things done. She draws from her emotions to manifest by using her heightened awareness. She is straightforward and committed. She will not go out of her way, however, to help you if you're being whiney, which is odd because we usually think of the Cups as being the touchy-feely suit. This is because the Queen of Cups is about spirit energy and compassion, not about romantic or motherly love. She energizes our crown chakra, as her task is to raise the energy of all those around her. She will help you feel connected again when you feel disconnected, empowered when you feel disenfranchised. She will help you raise your energy when you feel you can't go on; she will urge you to stand up for your beliefs and follow your dreams, but she will not coddle you, so don't go whining to her.

Reversed: It's hard to hear when you're underwater. When you get the Queen of Cups reversed it is time to swim back up through the murky depths and re-surface. You've probably gotten caught up in an emotional undersea world. You may not feel at home in the world above, but you really don't belong underwater either, and if you stay down there much longer you may end up swimming into a net and really getting caught up. If you can, use your emotional energy to enhance your psychic energy and allow yourself to float to the surface. You may have blocks to raising your energy, but if you relax, your spirits will be lifted, and that will start your ascent back into the light.

The Knight of Cups

KNIGHT of CUPS

Keyword: Expanding
Chakra: Root, Red

Dolphins are sacred to many seafaring peoples. They were sacred to the Hawaiians, the Finns and the Celts. The dolphin is a symbol of transcendence, metamorphosis or change.

The Greek myth of Arion, as told by Herodotus and Plutarch, is an example of sacrifice and transformation. Arion, a great musician, was on his way home by sea after winning a musical contest. Pirates decided to take his winnings and his life, but they granted his last request of playing his lyre for Apollo before being put to death. With his last note, he dove headlong into the sea to spare himself the disgrace of capture. He fully expected to drown, but rather than drowning, he was borne up on the back of a dolphin who had heard the music.

The allegory illustrates that if we let go of that which is dearest to us, in this case Arion's prize money and his life, we may not lose it after all – it may end up transformed. Said in another way, the old axiom "if you love it, set it free" holds true. In the end, Arion transforms into a demigod, and he has the pleasure of banishing the pirates from the kingdom where they take his winnings for trade. His life, music and treasure are restored. The Knight of Cups invites you to be fearless, take the emotional risk and dive headlong into the deepest waters of your own emotional abyss. You are a buoyant being, and more resilient than you think. Emotional change often begins with grieving or sinking to the bottom. Once you touch bottom, though, there's nothing left to do but to float back up to the top.

Healing can take place even when you feel you are at your least serene. During the First Crusades of Pope Urban II, begun in 1095, hordes of mercenaries invaded the Middle East.

It was a Christian assault on the Muslim countries to expand the Roman Catholic Empire and reclaim Jerusalem. By 1099 the Christians finally won the day from the Seljuq Turks, and as the Christian settlement expanded, the Order of St. Lazarus of Jerusalem was established to treat virulent diseases such as leprosy. Like most colonization stories, this one ends with the demise of the invader about 200 years later, but within that time of harsh invasion and truculent cultural expansion there were humanitarian ventures that prevented implosion.

That which seems most violent can be masking a greater good taking place under the surface, and allowing it to transform us is our task. The root chakra is used in this card because of the fundamental foundation of feeling associated in family and tribe. Feeling safe and provided for allows the Knight of Cups to swim beyond his emotional safety zone. He can express his emotions thoroughly. When you get this card do not drown in your emotions, rather be uplifted by your ability to feel so deeply. Transform yourself, feel your feelings, but know that you can transcend any sorrow or anger by expanding your feelings of compassion and gratitude. In an explosion of joy, the dolphin leaps up into the air with the Knight of Cups on his 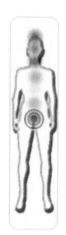 back. The Knight has his cup extended, reaching for the stars. They revel in the gratification springing from their unity as divine beings, their bond founded in peace, friendship and brotherly love.

Reversed: You're treading emotional waters, and it is exhausting your ability to feel at all. It is okay to feel things like sadness, fear, rejection and anxiety, but it isn't okay to let bad feelings control you. In English, the problem is partly built into the language linguistically. It leads us to think that we are our feelings, but we are not. The Knight of Cups says to replace "I am angry" with "I feel angry." This creates distance from being and feeling, and it creates a more accurate statement. The statement allows you to feel it, but you simultaneously identify that "you" are not actually "the feeling." You are not your emotions. If you are able to replace feelings of anguish with small feelings of joy, do so. Enjoy a walk, or just sit still in the sun. Find a way to allow yourself to feel again. If you need a good cry, go for it. But don't lose yourself to sorrow; there is too much good in you to do that, and remember to identify your feelings as feelings. There are many techniques for letting go of unwanted emotions. When you find one that feels right for you, use it, but remember that you need to replace the bad feelings with good because nature abhors a vacuum. Your psyche will go back to what is familiar if you're not vigilant, so fill your heart with love and float in your emotional waters instead of struggling.

Page of Cups

Keyword: Poetic
Chakra: Solar Plexus, Yellow

Steam rises from the golden caldron delicately balanced on its rocker. The green woman is a young earth sprite in a light blue cloak. She touches down gracefully on one toe near the steaming cauldron, leaving it undisturbed. The cup of hot liquid is teetering on the edge – one false move and it will spill its contents of unsettled swirling emotion. The Page of Cups must be very careful in her approach towards inner wisdom. Her methods are poetic, artistic and deep. She is all too aware that if she tips the cup too far one way or the other the contents will spill, and her new-found emotional wisdom will be lost.

From the Page of Cups a new form of creative consciousness, inspiration, or an unexpected connection to the divine is in the works for you. Expect to experience dreams with messages, déjà vu, or odd impulses that lead to synchronicity. The Page of Cups is a lovable, graceful, and overly sensitive individual. In most situations, she is the highly charged person who changes the dynamic in the room from lively to reflective. It isn't her intent to be so intense; she just gives off that vibe because she is often given to silence.

When you get the Page of Cups it means a time of turmoil has ended and a new layer of emotional enlightenment is coming into being as a new perspective. Make your own poetic brew of coffee, tea or chocolate and imbibe in the warmth of the steamy liquid. Allow it to act as a reminder that warm contentment and a soothing nature come with emotional self-knowledge and balance.

Reversed: The sensitive nature of the Page of Cups has teetered over into emotional overload. You or whoever the

Page of Cups represents is acting immaturely, to say the least. Emotional outbursts, inappropriate behavior, and lack of sociability are all characterized by this card, but the underlying cause is more than likely lack of self-love and self-acceptance. Feeling rejected or hurt often leads to escapism. Emotional equilibrium is not something that we usually consciously strive to attain, but we recognize it when we see it; conversely, we recognize the emotionally wounded as well. For good or ill, we're drawn to that with which we vibrate most. If you find that you are the caretaker too often, and that you feel depleted in your dealings, you might be drawn to people who are unable to conduct healthy relationships. That said, you might want to take a step back and do a little self-reflection. The caldron of inner knowing may cloud your vision and may sting your tongue at first, but if you sip gently, you will find that the potion quenches your thirst for love and warmth. Seek emotional stability through self love.

Ten of Cups

Keyword: Contentment
Chakra: Crown, Violet

Gratitude springs from spirituality, fulfillment, peace, friendship and brotherly love. If the waters pouring forth from the Ten of Cups were frozen and photographed through an electron microscope, they would yield crystals like those found in Masaru Emoto's "love and gratitude" photographs in his book *Hidden Messages in Water.*[26] You are abundant in good vibes; your molecular structure is vibrating at a very high frequency - allow yourself to experience peace and gratitude.

You have in some measure attained the perfection of "flow." An abundance of energy is at your disposal. In fact, you should expect an 'overflow' of pleasure and satisfaction. Just as the image illustrates, an overflow of emotion is presenting itself when you get this card. Be aware that this is the peak of the bell curve. That is not to say that everything is downhill from here, but that you have done as much as you can in this matter. You should be satisfied with what you've done, relish the wealth of experience that life offers. Enjoy it. Most often this card is associated with good feelings. But it can also indicate simply an over-abundance of emotion and feeling.

The energy of the Crown chakra flows from the top of the head, showering a pyramid of white light energy down into the depths of each chakra below. Joyous, harmonious vibration is effortless, and growth is assured simply by virtue of being. Enjoy the flow of life and embrace contentment and gratification.

Reversed: Ten of Cups reversed indicates either blocks in being able to experience feeling and emotion or feeling too much. It indicates extremes in one direction or the other. Either way you are experiencing a dampening of your energy field. If you are feeling depressed, find a way to get to the heart of what is depressing you, or maybe increase your exercise level to awaken your body. Simple disassociation of body and mind can cause a depressed state because of the lack of serotonin or dopamine in the brain. One thing you can do to increase these pleasure hormones is to exercise, but if there is really something wrong, you'll need medical advice.

Getting the Ten of Cups reversed could conversely indicate you're taking the logical approach a little too literally and denying your feelings about something that is actually quite important to you. Examining our true feelings about someone or a situation can be draining, but denying our emotions will lead to poor health. Examining our inner needs will lead to release, which is much healthier. Whatever it is that is holding you back from enjoying living your life, find a way to connect with your true feelings, but also find ways to increase joy in your life.

Nine of Cups

NINE of CUPS

Keyword: Fulfillment
Chakra: Heart, Green

Nine is the number of the celestial spheres, Zeus's muses, and the planes of heaven in Dante's *Divine Comedy*. Dante also considered nine the number of love, assigning it as Beatrice's number in his Paradiso. In Celtic myth, the Salmon of Knowledge gains his insight into the world because he eats the nine hazel nuts that fall into the Fountain of Wisdom from the nine hazel trees that surrounded the fountain. In Chinese numerology, nine is the number of fulfillment and the Yang principle.

In the painting's background, behind the glass shelves holding nine glass goblets, a serpent dragon sits; he is a symbol of fulfillment and completed manifestation. In Chinese mythology, his ejaculate serves as the primeval waters for the world egg. The dragon is associated with the *Tao te Ching*, (*Book of Changes*,) and his blood is black (earth) and yellow (heaven). He embodies the six stages of manifestation from 'hidden dragon' (potential) to 'swooping dragon' (flying forth), holding the essence of manifestation and immortality. The Hindu also consider the dragon an immortal water creature. The concept of prajapati or 'first cause' is the dragon's waters (sperm) called 'soma,' and it is the drink of immortality. In the myth of Yu the Great, Yu drained the floods of the world into nine caldrons, setting the world right once more.

In an additional dragon myth, the 'dragon's pearl' is held in the dragon's throat, and is conferred upon those who have mastered perfection of thought and speech.

As humans, we are nine months in gestation; remember that nine is love and perfection. When you get this card, drink from the nine cups and swallow the perfection into your heart. Say what you mean and mean what you say in order to experience the jewel of fulfillment.

Reversed: A reversal in the Nine of Cups indicates feeling unfulfilled. You're frustrated by things not going as you'd like. It could be there are extenuating circumstances preventing your realizing your dreams or it could be because of internal conflicts. Whatever the case, we have blocked emotional (cups) fulfillment (nine), and when the card is reversed, it means the energy is muted or blocked in some way. So you're lacking in emotional fulfillment. The dragon within holds your potential and will help you manifest what you desire. Consider perfecting your thought and speech to match who you really intend on becoming. Frustrations, especially emotional frustrations, are often obstacles that teach us lessons about our strengths and weaknesses. These life lessons offer us opportunities to develop coping mechanisms that we can use later in life.

Eight of Cups

EIGHT of CUPS

Keyword: Sharing
Chakra: Sacral, Orange

In some other Tarot sets, this card is rather downtrodden, represented by an inability to hold energy, by a pox, or by a depressed state of mind. White Light Tarot takes this idea but expands it from illness alone to include a healing motif.

The dolphin and killer whale share the waters, an infinity symbol as their hoop. Note that this symbol is also a sideways eight, hence the use of the symbol for the Eight of Cups. Through continual motion, they keep the waters energetic, and a vortex of healing energy forms. The pox is dissolved by the sea, and by sharing the load, the finned mammals demonstrate that together, we can harness more energy rapidly. When you are feeling demoralized, plagued by life's pace, find others that will share the load, and bathe in the healing waters that are generated by a healthy exchange of help and nurturing. Meditate with our cousins - the mammals of the sea. Do not let the oppressive thick energy of emotion weigh you down. Instead stay energetic and swim through life's hoops joyfully. Share the burden with those who love you.

If you feel alone, mentally call upon dolphin and whale to come to your aid. Seafaring cultures have many stories about mermaids, dolphins and seals. There are stories of transformation, and stories of sacrifice, all with the aim of teaching us to understand and appreciate love. There are stories of rescue and challenge that invite us to explore the deep dark waters of fear and freedom. Let the archetypes of dolphin and whale pull you to shore. You have infinite power to love; begin by acknowledging your vulnerability.

There is one more symbol to consider when you get this card because the eight golden cups represent the phases of the moon. The moon is our best guide for remembering that there are phases to everything in life. The moon grows from shadow into a full lighthouse beacon in a mere 28 days. Use this time frame as a reminder that we are sojourners in this life, and the world is for us to share. Take part in life and remember that when something feels oppressive, it is just a phase. Find others to share the load, and the time will pass more quickly.

Reversed: You're discontented and ready to chuck it in, but that may be because you're trying to do it all yourself. If you're feeling unappreciated, take a look at how you treat others. You may think it's reasonable to expect the same from others as you do from yourself, but look at how you treat yourself. If you are judgmental and angry that nothing is going your way, you might consider rethinking your approach. You'll attract more flies with honey than with vinegar as the saying goes. Endeavor to share what you really think and who you really are without oppressing others. You are vulnerable and human, just like everyone else. Allow yourself to ask accordingly.

Seven of Cups

SEVEN OF CUPS

Keyword: Connection
Chakra: Brow, Indigo

Global communication is how we live today. The Seven of Cups is represented as satellite dishes radiating their beams to connect with other satellite dishes in a worldwide relay. When we are too caught up in the broadcast news, it can be overwhelming. Information, just like anything else, can become an addiction.

CNN, Weekly World News, BBC, Tokyo Broadcast System (TBS), China Today, and Global Broadcast News (GBN) in India – all represent the wealth of information available to us today. All offer us interconnected choices in how we receive and eventually perceive our world. This can lead to overload, but it can also mask escapist behavior. World politics offers an escape from our individual boredom, loneliness and desires. We can rationalize our behavior in the name of political concern. It offers a handy disguise that one can brandish as a badge of honor when, in reality, nagging negligence of personal relationships, interpersonal skills and self care are hidden beneath.

How we filter general knowledge informs our everyday decisions, and our decisions foster our world view. Our decisions also help us realize our dreams, so be very careful about how much you imbibe at the abundant font of information. As with anything you drink, too large a quantity or too poor a quality can be bad for you, so moderation and quality control are needed. Be careful about the source.

We cannot live in a fantasy world, nor can we live in a world devoid of contact, but there are limits on how much information we can process and use wisely. If you allow the news to dominate your world view, you may sacrifice your own desires. In your pursuit of true meaning you may end up submitting to someone else's agenda. This is not to say you should not do good works, or pay attention to world situations, it is just to reinforce that we all must choose wisely when giving away our time and energy. Moderation in all things is the wisest course.

Reversed: Let the knowledge wash over you, soak in what you can, harness our burgeoning globalization and relish the good aspects of communication and camaraderie, then release what you do not need back into the cosmos. The information will return when you need it, have no doubt. You will always find the information or connections that you require, if you keep looking, and stay open to the abundance available to you. We are all connected and we vibrate at similar frequencies in and out of sync, in rhythm with the earth. If you are feeling out of sync, it will pass; concentrate on your psychic connection to what you value most at this moment.

Six of Cups

freedom

SIX OF CUPS

Keyword: Freedom
Chakra: Throat, Light-Blue
Unconventional cups to be sure, as these cups are distant golden birds flying over a turbulent sea at dawn. Soaring high above the fantastically deep and rich waters of emotion, these birds offer us clarity of scope in our approach to life's problems. Find a way to express your inner soaring spirit flying high above any choppy sea of emotional waves. Nothing matters more than allowing your spirit to soar. Communicate your inner wealth of joy and experience the emotional freedom that is your birthright.

When you get this card you are riding a wave of excitement and ecstatic release that the Six of Cups represents. The Six of Cups says you should communicate your joyfulness with abandon. In David Rothenberg's book *Why Birds Sing: A Journey through the Mystery of Bird Song*, the author conducts experiments where he plays jazz riffs to birds. He later discovers that certain phrases begin to propagate through their songs. As they play it back and forth to each other, like jazz musicians, the birds begin to riff on the phrases as well. The various species speak to each other, expecting a return response; they relay not only location and mating status but Rothenberg hypothesizes that birds sing for the joy of singing. In the Six of Cups the feeling of the card is one of exuberance, and like in Peter Pan's "I Gotta Crow" you should be ready to communicate exactly who you are fearlessly. Express yourself freely; dance, sing, write, live and enjoy.

Reversed: When we are feeling stuck or oppressed, sometimes it can be due to our surroundings or other people, but often it is because of own internal dialogues that are harsh and judgmental. If you are feeling like you cannot be who you want to be without some major sacrifice in your life, then it may be time to take flight away from the situation that is holding you down. You may need to free yourself from some situation, or person, or create an internal interrupt that can help dissolve harsh inner dialogs. Problematic inner dialog will not vanish even if you change your external circumstances, but change can help you build new connections that will allow you to flourish.

In pelagic bird colonies during the mating season it is very crowded on the small rocky shores where the birds raise their hatchlings. But without the support of those around them, the birds would be vulnerable to attack. There is strength in numbers and birds of a feather flock together. You will find the place where you are comfortable and where you belong. There are people who will accept you for who you are, but you might have to keep flying solo until you find them. Then you can soar together all the higher.

Five of Cups

FIVE OF CUPS

Keyword: Disappointment
Chakra: Solar Plexus, Yellow

The Five of Cups is about disillusionment, discontent, loss, and disappointment. It is a difficult card to receive in a reading. Sometimes our expectations aren't met, and we feel cheated, slighted by the universe. When we become bitter, we are more easily broken. Confusion can also be an aspect of this card, as in not knowing how to read the situation, or not knowing which direction is the best course of action. When we are feeling a loss and moving toward bitterness and rage, we may need to sit with these feelings to process them, or we may need to find a constructive outlet. Do not turn them any farther inwards.

Getting a larger perspective is needed to figure out what is wrong, and how to fix it. The cup can be half empty or half full; it's all a matter of perspective. If you are forced to drink the bitter dregs of disappointment, refill your cup with the milk of human kindness. If you feel you cannot rely on the kindness of others, then fill up on being kind to yourself. Take yourself out for a good meal, take a soothing bath with scented bath salts, take a walk in a favorite park, or simply watch a favorite movie -- do something to let your heart heal.

The Five of Cups, as with all fives, has a somber note to it. The energy of fives in the Tarot is one that lacks foundation and focus. It's the "Ricochet Rabbit" of energy, going "bing, bing, bing" back and forth in a never-ending formation. The energy has yet to be directed in any one way, and by inversion it is falling back on itself in an endless feedback loop. The figure looks down upon the glasses on the shelves in the window, each unique and separate. The window suggests a prison cell. Bars and separate cups represent compartmentalization. A survival skill in some regards in this modern world, we often compartmentalize our feelings and actions in order to continue on, instead of existing holistically. We are unable to act as an integrated being, which can lead to fragmentation and disillusionment. When you get this card, it is time to take positive action and find ways to integrate and invigorate your whole being. Try taking the glasses off the sills, dusting them off and putting them all on one tray. In other words, integrating your life from a single platform, a life harmonized and clear of any discordance, will help you find the direction that best suits your life right now.

Reversed: The energy is muted but it is essentially the same. When the Five of Cups comes up reversed in a reading, it is saying that some energy is not integrated. You are not acting with your full attention on some aspect of your life, which needs attention right now. To correct the situation try looking at your life in an overview perspective. If you were to take all of the glasses off the shelves and assign each a piece of your life, would there be enough glasses? If one is your relationship with your family, one with your primary relationship, one with work associates and so forth, are you integrated or compartmentalizing your life? Are you the same person in each situation? If you were the same person in each situation would things be different?

Four of Cups

Keyword: Tranquility
Chakra: Brow, Indigo

The Four of Cups uses four pink lotus blossoms to represent the cups rising from the murky water. Somewhat analogous to Adam, whom God formed from soft clay, the lotus comes from a fertile muck on the soft bottom of fresh water lakes and ponds and produces a flower that is likened to the soul. This card represents restfulness, and a quiet sense of belonging, but it also holds within it a reservation regarding the separation of our inner world of feeling (represented by the water where the flowers are rooted) and the outer world of actuality (represented by the air where the flowers blossom). Because of this co-mingling, there is a sense of limitation and stasis. It is hard work to keep these opposing forces continuously in balance.

As an emblem, the lotus is found in Asian, Hindu, and Egyptian art. It has a variety of meanings from overtly sexual to transcendent wisdom. Ultimately, it is a symbol of the life process, and each chakra is represented by a lotus flower. In Indian iconography, pink lotus blossoms are called "padma" and are considered the solar emblem of wealth.

The lotus appears pan-culturally in myth and literature. Examples include, *Odysseus* and the escape from the *Lotus-Eaters*, *Re* the Egyptian god who formed himself from a primeval lotus blossom, and *Horus the Child* who, seated on a lotus with his finger in his mouth in his youthful aspect, is the god of plenty and protection. The Buddha of Infinite Radiance is also known as the Padma-Pani or "Lotus Bearer" and Shiva, the Hindu god of transformation, turns himself into a lotus flower to escape harm in his guise as the mountain-goddess, Parvati.

In meditation, we often sit in the "lotus position," the cross legged sitting position that encourages open breathing and tranquility. The recognizable Tibetan chant "Om Mani Padme Hum" translates roughly to "Yea, Oh, jewel in the lotus! Amen." It is the Buddhist mantra of compassion, used in chant meditation to bring in tranquility and to seek the wisdom of the bo-dhisattva. The "Jewel in the Lotus" refers to our place in the universe as receptacle of karma (ac-tions) through dharma (proper conduct). When one reaches enlightenment, all illusion falls away and Nirvana emanates from the world axis, or center of the lotus blossom from within. When you get this card, focus your attention on the process of life and living it well, keeping your inner and outer worlds in balance and harmony.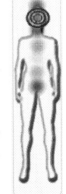

Reversed: Tranquil reflection and repose is great but too much can sometimes lead to complacency. If you find that you feel bored with everything and that you crave excite-ment, try to remember that it has not always been this calm. Be grateful for the silence in your life, because it gives you breathing room to re-create yourself as you really want. Re-member we are always in a state of "becoming"; nothing is really static or still. There is always some change happening; we just might not be able to see it. Bringing your thoughts from the depths of feeling out into the light takes practice. Try using the lotus blossoming as your focal point in medita-tion, representing your inner thoughts and feelings blossoming into reality.

Three of Cups

THREE OF CUPS

Keyword: Union
Chakra: Throat, Light-Blue

Achievement and abundance are headed your way. Celebrate by bonding with others and acknowledging your creative abundance. Relax and know that you are understood and appreciated. You just need to ask to join in the fun of life. If this card seems inappropriate to your situation right now, try looking at it from the vantage point of the cosmos. We are here for such a brief period. Shouldn't we celebrate and relish our time here? Communicate your feelings, whether they are good or bad, and celebrate that you feel so deeply; celebrate that you care. The etymology of the word 'celebrate' is related to gathering and grace, so a pleasant gathering is what this card depicts – the union of friends.

Inspired by Canova's "Three Graces" sculpture and Matisse's painting "Capuchines Dancing," the Three of Cups is an image of three women, each painted in a different style. A Sumerian-like woman hugs the Cubist-like woman in the center with a romantic nymph completing the triad. Joining the old and the new in layers, like the strata of the earth, building into a dynamic living organism, this image attempts to capture all of history in a single ideogram. Without knowledge of the past, we are doomed to repeat it. Remember that in celebration we give thanks to what has evolved, and what we have recently finished. Cherish the union you feel when you are with friends and celebrate your bright future together.

Reversed: When you feel ostracized from those closest to you, it can signal an internal rejection. Sometimes we have trouble connecting to others when we are too self-aware or not self-aware enough. Self consciousness can have disastrous effects on our ability to enjoy the company of other

171

people. Connecting one-on-one may be the place to start, and celebrate that you can feel deeply, but recognize that your feeling of being left out might be coming from within rather than from others. Genuine union feels great and is forgiving. You don't need to impress anyone. We all want to better ourselves, be acknowledged for our achievements, and be respected. When in doubt, confirm that you accept and respect yourself, and that you accept and respect others, and you'll notice that they'll do the same.

Two of Cups

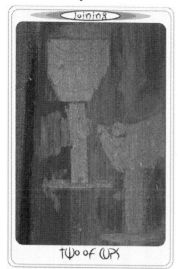

Joining

TWo of CUPS

Keyword: Joining
Chakra: Sacral, Orange

This card signifies the stable balance of give and take. The Two of Cups is associated with romantic love; you may be entering a friendship with someone of sexual interest and, if so, the relationship should be on an equal footing; that is, you feel the same way about each other. Enjoy the extra energy that joining forces with another creates. There may be interesting exchanges of yin and yang energies that will promote the "power of attraction,"[27] with the emphasis on creativity. Rejoice in the fusion that the Two of Cups represents. The White Light Tarot image incorporates the chakra colors to indicate intent. Violet and orange are a striking pair, opposites on the color wheel, but in energy work they are harmonious. The two colors connect creative and spiritual intentions. Join these chakras within yourself to create your most powerful vision for the future. Often this card means the beginning of romance or marriage, but it can also mean recognizing your creative spirit and following your spiritual intent.

Reversed: A word of caution regarding the idea "three is a crowd." You may be attracted to someone and entering into a friendship which could become significant romantically or creatively. Make sure you don't neglect your other friends in the process of pursuing new activities. Whether it's related to a platonic, business, romantic, or sexual relationship, the idea is partnership. Togetherness is celebrated, and a connection of some significance is imminent with someone or something in which you are interested, but be careful you don't go overboard. Easy does it, and en-joy your new association.

Ace of Cups

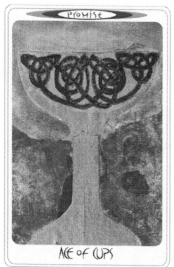

PROMISE

ACE OF CUPS

Keyword: Promise
Chakra: Root, Red

The Ace of Cups is related to the Horn of Plenty in that it contains the promise of your heart's desire. Nurture it. In Greek and Roman myth, Zeus is nursed by a divine goat as a baby, and then Zeus out of gratitude creates a Cornucopia from one of the goat's horns, which magically fills with what you want if you have the horn. In Celtic myth the Horn of Plenty is associated with fertility goddesses, and in Norse myth with Thor's drinking horn, and in one Native American tribe's stories, it is associated with rebirth.

In the White Light Tarot version of the Ace of Cups, the cup acts as the container for spiritual essence or soul. As you look into the cup, you see who you really are; you see your true self and your true potential, your fundamental nature as a loving being. Look deep into the glassy surface as it reflects your ability to give and receive love. Bring your face closer and examine the pools of your own eyes. Witness the depth of feeling reflected back at you, the caring, the pain, the love. This is the soul that you offer the world. If you are feeling world-weary or dried-up, drink deep from the cup and replenish your ability to nurture and receive.

Reversed: The Ace of Cups signals you have the ability to expand your heartfelt feelings, but you're not engaged in the process. Is the cup half empty or half full? Water is one of the elements that makes this earth and life possible. Water is a precious commodity. When you get this card, celebrate your ability to feel. Luxuriate in a steaming bath, walk in a lush garden, listen to music or simply have a goblet of wonderful fresh water to celebrate your fluidity. Replenish yourself.

THE DISKS

The Tarot's suit of disks is also known as the suit of pentacles, and it corresponds to the suit of spades in a conventional 52-card deck. The disks are about the physical, the material, or concrete world. While the other suits deal with the intellectual (swords), creative (wands), and emotional (cups) states of mind, the disks deal with the physical issues of being. The disks bring what we have imagined from intellectual curiosity through the creative passions into the emotional self and finally into concrete form. It is the end of the circle, if a circle can have an end. The disks are where we find the completed cycle of manifestation taking place. The element of earth is associated with grounding and disks. The disks are about bringing forth, growing, and yielding a harvest. The disks represent material goods, wealth, grounding, and bringing forth "from the ground up."

Just as the swords are associated with landowners (those with wealth enough to dedicate themselves to intellectual pursuits) and the wands with the "heathen" class (peasants), the disks are associated with the medieval merchant class. Finally, the cups are associated with those who dedicated their lives to God (or gods) and helping the needy, as exemplified in the clergy.

The King of Disks

KING OF DISKS

Keyword: Healer
Chakra: Crown, Violet

The king of disks is surrounded by a halo of green (love) energy. He calls in the earth's Reiki power as he creates a glowing ball of healing energy that he balances on the tip of his finger. Recent Japanese studies have confirmed that we emit light, especially from our fingertips and foreheads,[28] and that the emissions are rhythmic pulses. This pulsing demonstrates if nothing else that our heads and our hands are connected in a more powerful way than we usually acknowledge. By using our imaginations and our hands together, we can create powerful messages of what we want in our lives.

The King of Disks asks us to consider how we are using our hands. He invites us to sit down on the soft ground and begin to draw our dreams in the dirt. It's never too late to realize your dreams, he tells us. He invites us to begin by writing our hopes and dreams down, drawing them out and capturing them on a dream board. By making a dream board, you focus on what you want to happen. To make a dream board, first find images in magazines or on the internet that represent what you aspire to become, then pin them on a cork board near your bed so that you see them every day. By taking these actions you focus and energize your abilities to see your dreams through. Actualization is what the King of Disks is here to help you achieve.

The King of Disks is the shaman of the forest, gathering and dispersing earth's energy. He is most comfortable in a forest where it is easy for him to draw in elemental energies. The glowing ball is a physical manifestation of his healing ability. He can place this energy in you where it will transform and radiate warmth into the areas you need to heal. When you get this card, know that you can go to him at any time for a dose of paternal love. He will always be in the green forest of your heart, so seek him there. This card represents a nurturing and healing man in your life, or a part of the self that knows what you must do to heal any situation. He'll help you find your purpose, solidify your intention and animate your spirit. Follow his lead.

Reversed: You're not grounded and you're flitting about from one thing to the next. Until you can focus your energy, you'll feel as if you're running around in circles and getting nowhere. The King of Disks asks us, "What's the rush?" He invites us to sit down and chill out. Sometimes we need the soothing sound of a bubbling brook in the forest to reconnect to our mother earth. We need to get grounded. A little yoga can help if you can't get outside. Do the mountain pose by simply standing still. Do the corpse pose by lying down with your arms and legs uncrossed. The King of Disks reminds us that in order to manifest our dreams, we must first still our minds and hearts, release all worries and focus on our desires as if they were already manifested. Be happy.

The Queen of Disks

Keyword: Rescue
Chakra: Solar Plexus, Yellow

A warrior must understand the complexity of his surroundings. A warrior must instantaneously know what is most important, what to protect, and where to strike. The Queen of Disks is on a field of sunny green - a combination of love (green) and self-assuredness (yellow) surround her. She will protect you and the earth that she loves. She is attuned to her steed; they work in unison as one, effortlessly. The horse is a symbol in many cultures, sometimes representing a deity or a people, sometimes representing characteristics like speed and integrity. War horses figure prominently in the Book of Revelations and the horse represents either Christ or the Roman people, the symbol of independence, mobility and purity. The first written texts about the horse as a noble creature appear in Iran, dating back to 300 BC. Because horses are companions to us, they are loved and revered.

The Queen of Disks is genuine and generous, and she will rescue you without concern for her own well being. She has a mighty shield of love, and she has learned to harness the energy of others to her advantage. She does not take advantage of this ability, but only uses it if it is called for. She is keenly aware of how it can be used, so she is alert to false pretenses and manipulation. If she thinks that you're trying to manipulate the situation, she will knock you out like the queen in chess. She is the most powerful piece on the board, and she expects and deserves respect. Her shield of gold represents wealth and the energy of money, and her horse adds his speed and physical strength into the mix. She uses these tools to create her advantage, leading her cause to safety. If you lack self-esteem, she will lend you

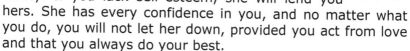

hers. She has every confidence in you, and no matter what you do, you will not let her down, provided you act from love and that you always do your best.

Reversed: You're not being genuine with what you want to do. You're capable enough, but you're facing resistance because you've fallen off your steed. The horse represents integrity. Be honest with yourself. What is most important to you? Act from that point. If you feel unsteady or unsure of yourself, call upon the Queen of Disks to help ground you and acknowledge your own power. She works with your solar plexus and helps to center you. You can learn or re-learn how to harness love without manipulation. You *do* know what is most important, what to protect and where to strike. Hesitation is human, but when you finally decide what you really want, the Queen of Disks will help you achieve it at full throttle.

The Knight of Disks

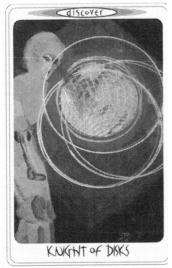

Keyword: Discover
Chakra: Throat, Light-Blue

This card breaks away from conventional Tarot, as the Knight of Disks is a female astronaut. Not bound by our earth, she examines the topography of another world displayed in a 3-D animation display, zeroing in on a new discovery. The silver rings of energy resonate and vibrate, keeping the visual display of the planet aloft. In a new take on old iconography, the White Light Tarot Knight of Disks remains the archetypal hunter – steady, quiet and strong – but she hunts for new information that will illuminate her understanding rather than hunting for sport or sustenance.

With focus and tenacity she examines her undiscovered country, and diligently documents her findings. She is very careful, and detail-oriented. She is methodical and steady, and although in this instance she is not in the earthly realm, she carries those roots deep inside her. So much so that she can leave the planet and take her earthbound rootedness with her, giving her great freedom to explore. What delights her most is digging into the depths of a subject and uncovering the crux of the matter. Figuring out how something works and explaining her discovery in a deliberate and demonstrative way is what the Knight of Disks loves most. She loves the green jewel called earth, and she carries that with her to new worlds. Call upon the Knight of Disks when you need to write a paper, examine legal documents, or confirm your findings. Call upon her when you need grounding and freedom to explore at the same time. She'll help you balance and focus, so that you can get the job done in the most practical way possible.

Reversed: Pay closer attention to details. Get grounded. You don't need to be in the grass to get grounded but it helps. When you get the Knight of Disks reversed, the message is to reconnect with the earth. You've become  sloppy and disinterested in maintaining things in working order. You may need to go back and start over, or at least to check your work. The Knight of Disks is telling you that you've lost your focus. To retrain your eye, take a deep breath, let it out slowly and have your feet firmly planted on the ground. Once you have grounded yourself, you'll be able to communicate what interests you much more clearly, and you'll find that people will listen more attentively when you are present and in the moment. This is the essence of grounding: connecting in the moment with what you are doing.

Page of Disks

PAGE of DISKS

Keyword: Empower
Chakra: Brow, Indigo

The Page of Disks has associations with the satyrs of Pan: he, too, is a mythical creature, but in this case, a centaur. He will grow to be like Chiron, tutor to Achilles, Hercules, and many other Greek heroes. Chiron was also a great healer, but he was killed by a poisoned arrow and he became the constellation of Sagittarius, the astrological sign of the philosophic mind. In the White Light Tarot image, the Page of Disks is the young Chiron, and we find him in the forest playing with a ball of energy. He has mastery of infinite source already, but being neither man nor beast he is fickle and sometimes forgets about his skills.

He is not one to concentrate to get things done, although he possesses the power to do so, he hasn't the desire. He is the consummate playmate at this young age, so do not rely on him. He will inspire and empower you to find your own way, but he will not sustain interest in solving any particular problems except for the challenge. Recognize him for what he is, and do not try to mold him into something he can never be, for he is not a whole man nor will he ever become a complete man. He is half beast, and will always be wild, and in a state of becoming. The Page of Disks is most comfortable in the shade of the cool green forest of earthly re-  sources. When you get this card, know that you have the skills necessary to achieve what you desire, but you must also have the discipline to see your dreams through to the end. When it is time, when you decide to, you will be able to stay the course and foster your dreams through to fruition.

THE DISKS

Reversed: The Page of Disks isn't bad; he's just playful and fidgety. He'll lead you away from your true ambition into the forgetful forest of fun if you let him. He'll lead you into the piney grove or the sacred circle of oaks to dances to Pan's pipes as much as any Satyr. He likes to party and he will keep you in a constant state of laughter, amusement and enjoyment. He loves to have a good time, but for us mortals life can spin out of control if we don't balance enjoyment with other aspects of life, like work and responsibility. Keep the Page of Disks as a playmate, but know that you'll need a little down time after the party is over. To get your groove back after the party in the grove, you'll probably need to meditate and release, so plan accordingly.

Ten of Disks

TEN of DISKS

Keyword: Delight
Chakra: Solar Plexus, Yellow

Early naturalists observed the bees' dance, noting communication, collective hive behavior and humming; therefore in myth, bees became an emblem of poetry, dance, song, and for some observers, like Plato, a metaphor for political society. For the Ten of Disks we'll concentrate on bees as a symbol of immortality and transformation. Bees symbolize immortality, possibly because we observed that without honeybees, we wouldn't live for long. We are reliant on bees pollinating at least 35% percent of the plant food we eat. There is evidence of hunter-gatherer tribes collecting orange blossom honey in Valencia, Spain 15,000 years ago. Cave paintings found in the region depict gathering honey. An additional reason for bees being a symbol of immortality could be the healing power of honey. Bees in myth relayed messages to and from the afterlife and the gods. The color and translucence of honey is reminiscent of gold, so honey is associated with wealth as well as longevity, and healing.

Honey is naturally antiseptic, and has amazing healing properties. It fights microbial fungi and bacteria, and it never goes bad. Honey was found in sealed jars in Tutankhamon's (King Tut's) 3,300-year-old tomb by Howard Carter in 1922. When the jars were opened, the honey was crystallized but not spoiled, and in 2007 more jars were discovered, amazingly still well preserved.

The figurative use of bees is similar in such diverse settings as South America, India, Egypt, China, Greece and

Europe. In many cultural rites, honey, mead, beeswax and bees played a role in rituals of transformation.

In White Light Tarot's version of the Ten of Disks we observe the delight of the bee on large globe grapes. The grapes represent a feast of forbidden fruit or spiritual knowledge not usually available to a mortal. If fermented, grapes will yield wine and for the Muslim Mystics like the Sufi poets red wine is "the drink of divine love." Red wine is also a metaphor for blood in some religious rites, and like its cousin, honey mead, when imbibed it confers a new form of understanding upon the initiate and a new way of expressing sexual and poetic voice.

The crux of the meaning of the Ten of Disks is that of a final transformation and delight in a treasured moment. That which was terrestrial changes back into the spirit. The transition is one of experience transmigrating into true wealth - the wealth of spirit. When you get the Ten of Disks it means you have achieved success and you have been able to transmute some form of spiritual energy (idea) into full fledged physical reality. The honeybee takes delight in using the grape's sweet juice to make her honey. Delight in your own ability to transform with her.

Reversed: Bees are natural messengers; they are sacred to Apollo. Apollo's son Aristaeus taught human beings how to cultivate bees and olives. In the last few years, we have cultivated the bees "out of business." Bees the world over have developed a syndrome that is known as Colony Collapse Disorder (CCD). The bees leave their hive, never to return, and as of yet, scientists do not understand what is causing this self-destructive behavior. Environmental stresses, pathogens, pesticides and parasites are all being investigated as causes, as well as genetically modified food crops like corn and soy. This is a worldwide message from the bees that something is wrong and something has got to change.

When you get the Ten of Disks reversed, you are becoming malformed in some manner. Take steps to correct how you behave and what you believe about yourself. You have the power to transform, but you must choose to change in the right direction. Take steps to let go of pathogens in your life, and you will be on your way to transforming your world for the better. When Napoleon took over France, he did not want to spend money redoing the palace, yet he refused to have the French Royal symbol of the fleur-de-lis on the draperies. "His solution was to have the rich and elegant drapes turned upside down. The inverted symbol of the overthrown monarchy looked like a bee. From then on, the tenacious bee became the emblem of Napoleon Bonaparte."[29] Maybe all you need to do is turn the way you look at things upside down.

Nine of Disks

Sustain

NINE of DISKS

Keyword: Sustain
Chakra: Heart, Green

The bicycle wheels represent your emotional ability to create. The wheels work together like a self-sustaining turbine, and the emotional turbine yields excess power that can be offered to others. Consequently, with the surplus of energy, and the bicycle wheels symbolizing evolutionary progress, this card represents a quickening of emotional development into the spiritual realm. You have created your life through a sustained focus of mind and psychic third-eye chakra. That means that when you set your mind to something, you can visualize it and achieve it. From this you've learned you can help others do the same thing. You are now acting from your heart center and in so doing you create a surge of energy into the crown chakra. You are prone to practice compassion towards others and you know the pleasure of satisfaction in your accomplishments and the accomplishments of others whom you foster with ease and ability. You understand how to be self-sustaining, effective and efficient. You can share your wealth of knowledge and techniques with others, or simply enjoy that satisfied feeling. If you decide to share yourself, you'll find even greater rewards await you. You offer a legacy of emotional maturity, kindness, and appreciation.

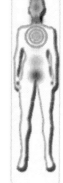

Reversed: In some emotional capacity, you are working well enough to generate excess power. Use your "emotional machine" to pump new life into all of your endeavors and share your power with others, as long as it isn't destructive. If you find your "emotional machine'" is mostly running on anger and steam, then change its focus to a productive endeavor. Don't vent at others, as that will only gum up the works. Keep your emotional turbines burning bright by developing your heart chakra. Practicing forgiveness and offering understanding to others and yourself is a good place to start. Keep spinning the spiral upwards towards your highest spiritual self.

Eight of Disks

EIGHT of DISKS

Keyword: Fruition
Chakra: Crown, Violet
  A cherry tree laden with fruit on a city block rises high above the fray. The tree demonstrates that beauty can prevail even in stressful circumstances. Trees in the city are not like trees in the forest. City trees are stressed out. Often gardeners have to help these non-native specimens with soil supplements, spraying and constant up-keep because the city is stressful for plants just as it is for humans and animals. Pollution, poor soil quality, lack of water and car exhaust fumes can wear a tree down, but despite it all they bloom beautifully. In the Eight of Disks we are shown a rather abstract version of the concept of fruition; still, the point is that of the final yield: you have risen above the ruckus and created something beautiful. What you have been trying to grow has finally come to harvest. Through great effort, trials and tribulations you've been able to cultivate something important.

  The sword of the Japanese Samurai is decorated with cherries and cherry blossoms to symbolize the growth of the invisible inner life. Cherries are considered a symbol of good luck in Japan. Japanese cherry blossoms come forth at spring equinox, sometimes when there is still snow, and the first fruit is ready by midsummer. In Japanese folklore, the wealth of the blossoms on the cherry was considered a foreshadowing of the health of the final harvest in the fall, and of the community at large. When you get the Eight of Disks, know that you are heading for a successful outcome. There are many things blossoming at this time.

Reversed: You are still growing, but you need help and nourishment to establish yourself well and stay strong. What you've done to date is great, but you need to continue to pay attention to detail and fine tune your work. When you are diligent and face your problems tenaciously, you'll find that you can accomplish a lot more than you thought. Keep at it, the harvest will come before you know it.

Seven of Disks

SEVEN of DISKS

Keyword: Limit
Chakra: Root, Red

The Seven of Disks shows an abstract interpretation of the proverbial is-the-jar-full paradox. A teacher asks a student whether a jar is full after placing small rocks in it up to the brim. The student replies that the jar is full. The teacher then adds smaller pebbles, shakes the jar, so that the pebbles fall between the cracks and asks again. The student says this time it is really full, but the teacher then adds sand which fills the jar even more. The point of the exercise is to demonstrate that we limit ourselves by definition. If we can expand our world view to include that which is unseen, or unknown, or, put another way, if we can learn to live with uncertainty, then we don't limit our capacity or capabilities. We are capable of more in some way. We can endeavor to be more giving, more thoughtful and more courageous. Alan Watts writes in the *Wisdom of Insecurity*:

"The timid mind shuts this window with a bang, and is silent and thoughtless about what it does not know in order to chatter the more about what it thinks it knows. It fills up the uncharted spaces with mere repetition of what has already been explored."[30]

Our minds are limited only by the strictures that we place upon them. Endeavor to undo what has been done to create the limitations that you are experiencing. Expand your horizons by seeing the world in a new and expanded way. Expand your lungs, expand your mind, expand and give in to no limitations.

Reversed: The jar has reached capacity, or has it? How many marbles are in the jar? That doesn't matter. What is essential is that although things may seem to have reached capacity, there is always room for more. If we add smaller marbles to the jar, if we add sand, if we add water, then we'll truly reach the limit of what the jar can hold. If you are feeling limited, or that you have reached your limit, look for different sources than you are used to using to help fill in the gap. When you get the Eight of Disks card know that your capacity is actually infinite. You can expand to include more than you might ever have imagined. So don't lose your marbles, just add other ways of doing things to get your life to feel full and fulfilling rather than overburdened.

Six of Disks

Six of Disks

Keyword: Strike
Chakra: Sacral, Orange

Evidence of the game of marbles has been found in Egypt, Greece, China and the Americas, and dates back 3000 years. In the classic game, your job is to knock your opponent's marbles out of the circle with your "knuckler." Your knuckler disperses the energy to the other marbles, sending any number of marbles to different strategic positions and out of the circle. Like Piaget's demonstration of the competitive and cooperative nature of stylistic learning, the marbles will in essence take a leader who will be the strike point. The strike point or knuckler is the prime mover who moves the energy through the group changing the dynamic of the crowd. You are the knuckler. Your next move is very important and can make or break the game. Create within your circle of friends or associates the momentum necessary to get things done. Set your strategy, and make your move. It is your time to strike.

The idea of patronage and karma (good deeds) is also associated with the Six of Disks, as is generosity. If you're not the one who is destined to strike and spread good fortune, then someone near you will offer their generosity towards you. They feel they owe you that much. You needn't feel indebted to others socially, psychologically, or spiritually any longer. If you are monetarily in debt, you should expect to find a way towards solvency with some help from others if you strike while the iron is hot.

195

Reversed: Your marble has been cast out of the circle and there may not be a way back into this game. That's okay; there is always the next round. When you get the Six of Disks reversed, you may have overreacted in some way. Carelessness with funds, emotions, food – in some manner you were either throwing caution to the wind or acting out of fear, or trying to impress someone with something beyond your means. You need to pull back and wait out the end of the game. There will be another chance to make up for lost ground, but next time, act strategically, generously, and for the good of all involved. Stay grounded and you'll find your way back into the game.

Five of Disks

FIVE OF DISKS

Keyword: Fleeting
Chakra: Throat, Light-Blue

The White Light Tarot image of the Five of Disks is an abstract expression of five peacock feathers on a vibrant red background, the color of pomegranate juice. The peacock and the pomegranate are both sacred symbols of Hera, the Queen mother goddess of Greek mythology, who was the deity that oversaw marriage and motherhood.

As Hera's emblem, the peacock is an insignia of pride, and the pomegranate is an emblem of marriage. Hera's chariot was pulled by peacocks, and the eye on the peacock feather was presented as a gift from Hera to Hermes for his fealty.

The Encyclopedia Mythica says, "It was Hermes who liberated Io, the lover of Zeus, from the hundred-eyed giant Argus, who had been ordered by Hera, the jealous wife of Zeus, to watch over her. Hermes charmed the giant with his flute, and while Argos slept Hermes cut off his head and released Io. Hera, as a gesture of thanks to her loyal servant, scattered the hundred eyes of Argus over the tail of a peacock (Hera's sacred bird)."[31]

The eyes of the peacock feathers represent an omniscient eye that we all have – an internal knowing. Energetically, you have all the tools you need to live life to the fullest, but you must recognize that this life is fleeting and you are responsible for your feelings and reactions. The Five of Disks is a warning against hubris, or arrogance. Taking pride in yourself and what you are married to (meaning what you hold dear) is part of being a whole person, and experiencing the human condition. But sometimes we get caught in a trap of identifying ourselves with what we do for a living or what we believe or our associations - the keeping up with the Joneses mentality. When that happens, we are no longer truly reacting as ourselves; we are reacting as the image of ourselves.

When you get the Five of Disks, you may feel insecure for some reason, or energetically impoverished in some measure, but this is temporary. Remember that the nature of who you are and what you do is fleeting. Stay aware of your feelings, be present and communicate them as well as you can, every chance you get. Remind yourself that you are whole, regardless of what you may feel. Remind yourself that life is fleeting even if you feel you have a lifetime.

The Penguin Dictionary of Symbols says, "In esoteric tradition, the peacock is a symbol of wholeness, in that it combines all colors when it spreads out its tail in a fan. It exhibits the intrinsic identity of short lived nature of all manifestation since its forms appear and vanish as swiftly as the peacock displays and furls its tail."

This is the paradox of human existence. We often feel the opposite of what is really true. This is our collective hubris as, in reality, our time on earth is short lived, and we already have everything that we need to live life fully.

Reversed: The Five of Disks reversed means essentially the same thing that the Five of Disks means right-side up. Life is fleeting, so don't get hung up on material worries. This too shall pass. In the medieval morality play, *Everyman*, the character Death tells Everyman that time waits for no man (."..the tide abideth no man..."). Death is telling Everyman, "rely on yourself and do good works, for you will be held accountable for your actions in the eyes of God." The Five of Disks says you are whole, sound and a complete work of beauty unique in the universe - don't feel sorry for yourself, find a way to celebrate life, because that is why we're here.

Four of Disks

FOUR of DISKS

Keyword: Recharge
Chakra: Root, Red

Recuperation is what is required. You've pushed yourself, so now you have what you need, but you're on the edge of becoming overwhelmed with striving. If it continues this way, you'll end up greedy. The four globes cycle above the sacral and root chakras of the prone figure to recharge the areas of creativity and stability. Take a moment to enjoy what you have achieved and recognize that without recharging your batteries every now and again, you're no good to yourself or to anyone else.

Fours are about stability and order, and the Four of Disks is especially about material wealth. Hoarding your energies will not help you achieve further abundance. Hoarding only leads to stagnation. The equal exchange of energy is what is required, financial as well as emotional and spiritual. Frugality and conservation are not the enemy; it is the feeling that we lack something – the feeling that there is never enough '_____' to go around (fill in the blank with love, time, money, friends whatever). If you feel neglected in some way, or lacking in love, approval or self worth then you may need to recharge your batteries and give to yourself for a little while.

When you get the Four of Disks it indicates that you have pushed yourself to the point of exhaustion and that you are becoming miserly with your time, energy and monies. Take time to reflect on your feelings about abundance. Being protective is okay, but if getting the Four of Disks indicates that you have been giving too much, pull back a bit for your health. After determining why you are drained, you can begin to recoup any losses you may have incurred. It may require that you to slow down and reorganize your thinking. Know that in the order of things, its okay for you to take the time you need to restore your energies, redress and recuperate. Give yourself permission to relax.

Reversed: When you get the Four of Disks reversed it indicates one of two extremes. Either it is time to let go of the security blanket and get on with it, or you've been wasteful with your resources. If you've been micromanaging your existence then it is time to allow some flexibility and spontaneity into your life. Take a step out into the world, and experience new choices and synchronicities. You have the stability, security and creativity to achieve what you want. Go for it.

On the other hand you may need to stop wasting time and thinking of shopping as a recreational sport. Often when we go overboard with spending money it is to make up for some lack in another area in our lives. Find a way to appreciate what you have and give back to others in a way that will help you regain your equilibrium. It's time for a change and a little conservation.

Three of Disks

THREE OF DISKS

Keyword: Work
Chakra: Sacral, Orange

Three silver disks are connected by energetic lines of green as a dynamic exchange of love energy is taking place. The disks work together to establish equilibrium, together creating more energy than any of them could alone. The circular connection spurs a spiral of expanding upward energy.

In both the Eastern Tantric and Western Hermetic alchemical traditions, three is the perfect number. Paracelsus referred to this trinity as the Tria Prima or the Three Prime Elements, but the word 'elements' acts as a stand-in for principles as well as substances. As principles, Mercury ($\mathived$) supplies connectivity; it's the go-between, Sulfur ($\mathived$) that acts as the binder. It keeps things together long enough for Salt ($\mathived$) to act as the solidifying agent. As a person transforms, Mercury represents the spirit, Sulfur is the passion or emotional force, and Salt is the body.

When you get the Three of Disks, either you are working on a transformation or your work life is ramping up in some way, and may include others in the process. Use the concept of the three prime elements to heighten and hasten the development. On your favorite windowsill, use a piece of silver or a coin to represent mercury. The silver represents communicating with spirit and quickening or speeding the process to fulfillment. Add a yellow citrine stone to represent sulfur for manifestation, and add a pinch of salt for clearing and grounding. Get to work on manifesting your dreams, and remember that things usually happen in threes.

201

Reversed: If you hate your work then it is time to find a way to move on. This process can be very time-consuming and arduous, but the rewards are worth the effort. Admittedly, sometimes we have to work at a job that isn't our ideal, but that doesn't mean that we should give up on the possibility of finding work that suits us better. Without working towards a goal you believe in, you deplete yourself and find that you have less and less energy to offer. Find a way to reward yourself for your efforts, and remember that to a certain extent you can change your work environment by changing your attitude. That's not to say you should simply play Pollyanna, or drink yourself stupid, but that you should put your situation in a greater context, set a goal of getting to the next level or out of your current arrangement and find ways to encourage yourself to take action. If there's no way that you can make money doing what you're passionate about, then at least find a way to fit it in on the side. Reignite passion in your life so that you don't miss out on transformative opportunities and experiences. Find something that you enjoy doing and put some effort into doing it, work at it. Sometimes that's all it takes to get things moving.

Two of Disks

Keyword: Channel
Chakra: Brow, Indigo

In the White Light Tarot Two of Disks, a young man kneels in a pool of possibility, drawing in energy to create his ideal life. When you get the Two of Disks, recognize yourself as an energetic being, and welcome the possibility of a more vibrant and successful you. Be adaptive, channeling your psychic energy to create the person you wish to become. The Two of Disks indicates that right now you are capable of harnessing and utilizing the vibrancy of the world. Enhance your ability to create your ideal life by finding out what you want most. What makes you happy? What challenges you? What are you willing to juggle? Go to concerts, plays and events, read the paper, participate in group activities, and spend time daydreaming to uncover your true desires. Whatever it is that you want, focus your energies on creating an environment that welcomes that thing or energy.

It is probably true that the more you know, the more you can influence, but being flexible and adaptive are just as important as book smarts. This is a high energy card, that of the creative channel. You are able to juggle the tasks set before you efficiently and effectively, but you should keep learning and choose wisely. It is easy to get overwhelmed when you have either a lot of energy or a lot to get done. The Two of Disks says you're able to face life's challenges with confidence and adaptability; continue to channel your energy wisely.

Reversed: What are you afraid of becoming? Worry is a form of focus. When you worry about something you're giving it more energy. If you're familiar with *What the Bleep Do We Know?!* then you are familiar with the idea that what we think can influence our surroundings. We are undoubtedly more than the sum of our parts, but proving it can be daunting. We still live in a skeptical society that doesn't easily embrace that which cannot be seen or proved scientifically. That said, most science was considered magic, heresy or pseudoscience at one point or another, so believe in yourself and influence your world by focusing on what you want and what you can influence, rather than on what you don't want or can't do anything about. For example, worrying about polar bears and global warming isn't going to help the bears, but turning off the lights when you leave the room will have an impact on how much energy you consume, which in a small way, will help the bears. In this way you can affect change with constructive action. Small actions can lead to great benefits. The Two of Disks reversed is a warning against putting energy into the wrong things.

Ace of Disks

Keyword: Prosper
Chakra: Heart, Green

Prospects are good that when you get the Ace of Disks you are going to prosper and enjoy good fortune and success. You are at the beginning of a new phase of life physically or materially. The shape of a dodecahedron is based on phi-ratio geometry and it represents energy spiraling upwards, like molecules using the five-sided vertex of the dodecahedron to bind DNA; you are building from the inside out.

The virtue of any geometric symbol is built upon Pythagoras's theorem of the golden number, or Fabonacci's Golden Ratio *Phi* Φ of divine proportion; it boils down to the underlying principle that everything has infinite spiraling activity. This means we all break down into fractals, and it offers some credence to the notion that we can energetically influence our surroundings by what we concentrate on and think about.

Accordingly, the dodecahedron pictured in the Ace of Disks is traced from Leonardo Di Vinci's notebook entries on the perfection of the universe. This geometric shape is famed for its beneficial qualities, like those of the pentagram; it evokes psychological responses that start the energetic flow of prosperity effortlessly.

Plato's dialogue *Timaeus* (c.360 B.C) discusses the constitution of each geometric shape or "platonic solid" and associates each with an element. The dodecahedron is associated with ether, the fifth element that of spirit, and it was also a symbol for the universe.

Though hotly debated, suggestions have been made that the shape of the universe is a finite dodecahedron, and it is interesting to note that ancient texts support many of these suppositions that are being proven out in astrophysics in the 21st century. As *Star Trek*'s Mr. Spock says, "Live long, and prosper." (Sorry, I just couldn't resist.)

Reversed: The dodecahedron is a symbol for the development of the universe, and it is possibly the true shape of our planet. Planetary grid theorists suggest that earth's magnetic field and the earth itself is "a crystal-like icosa-dodecahedral fractal," and discernable planetary collapse is traceable because of changes in the shape and vibrancy of biospheric processes and changes in magnetism being brought on by global industrialization. Maybe you need to look at your immediate environment and decide if it is inversely affecting your spirit and your energetic spiral upwards.

Use the Ace of Disks as a visual reference in meditation. The dodecahedron is made up of 12 pentagons, and within each pentagon you can trace the lines of a pentacle, or a sphere, or a square, or a triangle - hence it holds 'all,' and to contemplate the *all* is to contemplate the divine. Contemplate your divinity and your place in our divine universe.

THE SEVEN MAJOR CHAKRAS

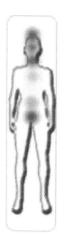

The chakra energy system is comprised of seven major energy centers that run up and down the spine. Each governs certain aspects of health. "Each chakra is believed to be a spinning wheel of energy: chakra means 'spinning wheel' in Sanskrit, where the *prana*, or life-force, of the body is held and organized."[32]

We start with the Crown chakra and make our way down the body to the base of the spine to the Root chakra. At the end of each chakra entry there is a list of corresponding Tarot cards.

Violet - Crown chakra, spirit
Sahasrara

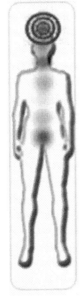

The Crown chakra (Sahasrara) is the seat of higher consciousness and the master chakra of the body. The Crown chakra is associated with the thalamus and pineal glands' role in physiological-psychic phenomena.[33]

Release of old patterns, effortless manifestation, intuitive understanding, and compassion are controlled by this chakra.

If this chakra is out of alignment, we may have trouble sympathizing, or feeling compassionate toward others. We may not see our role in the greater scheme of things and our worldview may be narrow in scope. We may feel victimized, and fated to some given end. General problems with the Crown chakra out of alignment are anxiety, not sleeping well, or a general feeling of persecution and anger. Demanding that reason and logic dictate everything can lead to frustration and headaches that could also indicate that the Crown chakra is out of balance.

To help regulate this area meditate intoning the sound of 'OM,' and visualize white light or violet light streaming into the top of your head. You might want to use visual stimulus props like amethyst crystals for visual concentration and scents like violets or lavender for aromatherapy.

Properties of a Balanced 7th Chakra
- Open to divine direction
- Compassionate awareness
- Tapped into subconscious
- Tapped into unconscious archetypal mind
- Inspired knowing

Violet was once the color reserved for Roman, Egyptian and Persian royals, and it was considered the color of blood. Greek myth credits Hercules, or rather his dog, with discovering the dye, by chewing on a mouthful of snails along the Levantine coast. In the last days of Rome, the mollusk Murex was becoming scarce due to overfishing. Dyers reputedly smelled like dead fish, according to written accounts, but cloth dyed that color was worth its weight in gold. So smelling to high-heaven became the smell of wealth.

As mentioned earlier, white light is helpful in realigning this chakra as long as it is full spectrum. Sitting in the sun will restore and balance the ultra-violet spectrum, but be careful not to overdo it and wear appropriate sun gear and sunscreen. Practicing peace, love and understanding are the ultimate aids in developing our higher consciousness. Make the choice to live by higher principles and see how your perspective changes.

A number of Tarot cards are associated with the Crown Spirit chakra. These cards are associated with compassion, enlightenment, and consciousness.

CROWN CHAKRA ASSOCIATED TAROT CARDS & KEYWORDS

FOOL: ONENESS
DEATH: LIMITLESS
STAR: INSPIRATION
UNIVERSE: DIVINE LIGHT
QUEEN OF SWORDS: BEAUTY
NINE OF SWORDS: CRUELTY
NINE OF WANDS: ZENITH
ACE OF WANDS: FURNACE
QUEEN OF CUPS: RAISING ENERGY
TEN OF CUPS: CONTENTMENT
KING OF DISKS: HEALER

Indigo - Third-eye, brow chakra
Ajna

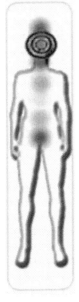

The Brow or third-eye Ajna chakra center is called the seat of spiritual knowledge. It governs our psychic awareness, and our ability to foresee things or visualize desired outcomes. It is the Clairvoyant-Intuitive part of our brain residing in the frontal lobe, which corresponds with our higher brain functions. Our ideas about reality and our ability to create that reality are derived from this chakra.

If this chakra is out of alignment, we may have trouble visualizing or seeing the big picture. We may get too caught up in detail and we "can't see the forest for the trees." We may chalk things up to fate or luck, but free will always plays a part in the creation of our circumstances, which are partly based on our world view. Social anxiety indicates a possible problem in the third-eye chakra. Conversely, needing to dominate or to control situations and others can indicate that this chakra is out of balance as well.

To harmonize this area, we need to practice self-appreciation, tolerance and love. Psychic energy is very powerful. Focusing your mind on how good life is, even through the rough times, will help you to vanquish many psychic and physical ailments.

Properties of a Balanced 6th Chakra
- We can visualize easily
- Sharp memory
- Intuition
- Quick reasoning ability
- Trust

The color associated with Ajna is dark midnight blue, or indigo. Vincent Van Gogh's painting *Starry Night* makes great use of that color.

To develop your intuition and third-eye chakra you can try meditating near a desert, ocean, or lake. Large vast expanses help to develop and soothe the mind at the same time. We open up when we are in great, vast natural spaces. Use a picture if you can't physically get somewhere expansive, or just look up at the night sky - it has the same effect. Expanse and expanding is the name of the game with this chakra.

A number of Tarot cards are associated with the Brow Third-eye chakra. These cards are associated with psychic ability, wisdom, and pure brainpower. If any of these cards come up in a Tarot reading, meditate on the ideas presented. Find ways to expand your mind and to help others see their true nature.

BROW THIRD-EYE CHAKRA ASSOCIATED TAROT CARDS & KEYWORDS

THE MAGICIAN: INTUITION
SACRIFICE (The hanged man): SELFLESSNESS
AWAKENING (Judgment): PSYCHIC
SIX OF SWORDS: INSIGHT
THREE OF SWORDS: SEPARATION
SIX OF WANDS: INWARD
FOUR OF WANDS: FORCE
SEVEN OF CUPS: INTUITION
FOUR OF CUPS: SELFLESSNESS
PAGE OF DISKS: PSYCHIC
TWO OF DISKS: INSIGHT

Light Blue - Throat chakra
Vishuddha

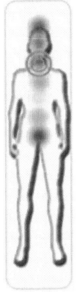

Vishuddha, the Throat chakra, is the color of ice blue cough drops. The Throat chakra is located just below the Adam's apple in the throat, and right around the thyroid gland which regulates our growth hormones. Associated with clarity and growth, this chakra governs our ability to express ourselves and communicate effectively.

Our inner voice and our abstract intuition (instant problem solving without formal logic) are derived from this area. If this chakra is over stimulated, we may suffer sore throats, feel we have something "stuck in our craw" or have a tendency to "run at the mouth." If it is under stimulated we may not be able to express ourselves with ease, and we may have a tendency to speak too softly, or strain our voice when trying to get a point across.

To regulate this area we can use the sound 'RAM' or 'RANG' in meditation. In Tibetan "Rang" means "self" and the goal is "rang tong" or to become "empty of self" to further enhance the experience of connection with all. We can strengthen this area by using sound generally; singing and chanting open the throat chakra.

Properties of a Balanced 5th Chakra
- Sound Conviction- One's words hold weight with others
- Confidence in the ability to express oneself
- Access to the Etheric communication[34]

Historically the color blue is associated with truth and fidelity as in the English idiom "he's true blue," or the folk rhyme "Married in blue, your love will always be true," which is where we get our something borrowed, something blue tradition. Hence, various shades of the color blue are used in advertising, business and the military to instill confidence in their message and ability to get the job done.

212

"In our society it seems as though one is always struggling to get their voice heard. When one has balance in the 5th center, an interesting coincidence is that one may find that their need to communicate with frequency reduces, but the power of their word increases." [35]

The Tarot cards that are associated with the Throat chakra will have to do with truth and communication, authority figures, archetypes, and actions always figure prominently.

THROAT CHAKRA ASSOCIATED TAROT CARDS WITH KEYWORDS

HIEROPHANT: WISDOM, KNOWLEDGE
JUSTICE: FEARLESS, EQUALITY
BALANCE: INTERCHANGE, HARMONY
PAGE OF SWORDS: MESSAGE
TWO OF SWORDS: TRUCE, TREATY
EIGHT OF WANDS: EMIT, EMANATE
TWO OF WANDS: STEADY
SIX OF CUPS: FREEDOM
THREE OF CUPS: UNION
KNIGHT OF DISKS: DISCOVER
FIVE OF DISKS: FLEETING

Green (and Pink) - Heart chakra
Anahata

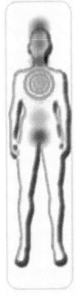

The Heart chakra (Anahata) is the seat of romantic love, affection, caring and compassion. This chakra is also associated with great strength and the ability to change. The Heart chakra governs our hands, heart, lungs and circulatory systems. It is our center of emotional balance.

If this chakra is under stimulated, we may suffer from indecision or fear of rejection and clinginess. If it is over stimulated, we may not be able to express love, and we mistakenly identify lust, longing, arrogance and power for love. When this chakra is out of balance, we will experience the lower natures of man, versus man's higher nature.

To regulate this area we can use the sound 'YAM' in meditation. Practicing meditation outdoors connects us with the color most associated with the Heart chakra. Surround yourself in nature to realign this chakra, and eat your greens.

Properties of a Balanced 4th Chakra
- Unconditional love for all
- Nurturing nature
- Confidence in love
- Mental layer of aura able to transmit and receive information effortlessly

A number of Tarot cards are associated with the Heart chakra. These cards are associated with love, devotion, connection, and compassion. If any of these cards come up in a Tarot reading, look for ways that you can associate with that card, such as situations in which you need to devote yourself, archetypes, and people you admire or love. Concentrate on the overall meaning of the spread, but always use your own images and associations that come to mind, as well. Trust your intuition.

214

HEART CHAKRA ASSOCIATED TAROT CARDS & KEYWORDS

LOVERS: DEVOTION
HERMIT: REALIZATION
WHEEL OF FORTUNE: CYCLES
EIGHT OF SWORDS: AFRAID
FOUR OF SWORDS: HARMONY
QUEEN OF WANDS: GENEROUS
THREE OF WANDS: BLISS
KING OF CUPS: SERENITY
NINE OF CUPS: FULFILLMENT
NINE OF DISKS: SUSTAIN
ACE OF DISKS: PROSPERITY

Yellow - Solar plexus, Navel chakra
Manipura

Manipura: the Navel chakra or the Solar Plexus chakra is located just above the belly button. This is the chakra of prana, or life force. For the Greeks, the solar plexus or diaphragm was "the seat of the soul,"[36] and the breath is a crucial way of controlling our body.

The Solar Plexus chakra governs our self-esteem, our confidence in ourselves, and our inner strength. Our ideas about how capable we are and our ability to create abundance are derived from this chakra.

If this chakra is out of alignment, we may physically have trouble "digesting a situation," or we may literally have an upset stomach or a queasy sense of uncertainty in our gut.

There are steps that we can take to help stabilize this area. The Solar Plexus responds to fire since it is the seat of our internal flame; it is our core, where we hold our highest concentration of life energy. Concentrate on a candle flame, or if possible dance around a bonfire outdoors to revitalize this area. Sitting in the sun will also restore the Solar Plexus chakra. Using yellow flowers in meditation like daffodils, sunflowers and Black-eyed Susans can help center you again. Wearing an amulet of amber, sunstone or citrine may help as well.

Properties of a Balanced 3rd Chakra
- See 'golden' opportunities
- Feel good about 'gut instincts'
- Self appreciation
- Tolerance of others
- Abundance

A number of Tarot cards are associated with the Solar Plexus chakra. These cards are associated with self-awareness, inner strength, and power. What you probably most need to work on when you are stressed or weak in this area is self-appreciation to increase the circulation and power of this area.

SOLAR PLEXUS CHAKRA ASSOCIATED TAROT CARDS WITH KEYWORDS

EMPEROR: FATHER, ACTION
CHARIOT: JOURNEY, STRIVING
TOWER: EXPLOSIVE, DESTRUCTION
KNIGHT OF SWORDS: DUTY, VALOR
ACE OF SWORDS: ACCURACY, EXACTING
PAGE OF WANDS: AMBITION, ABILITY
FIVE OF WANDS: IMPRISONED, ON HOLD
PAGE OF CUPS: POETIC, INTROSPECTION
FIVE OF CUPS: DISAPPOINTMENT, LOSS OF CONTROL
QUEEN OF DISKS: RESCUE, SUSTENANCE
TEN OF DISKS: DELIGHT, HAPPINESS

Orange - The sex center or Sacral chakra
Svadisthana

Located just below the belly button, the Sacral or sex center chakra governs our creativity and our sense of awe.

The Sacral chakra governs our ability to give and receive in all matters, including sexually and sensually. It is the seat of our sense of fulfillment, enjoyment and of course, procreation.

If this chakra is out of alignment, we may not recognize our own creative nature. We might feel undervalued or unappreciated in some aspect of our lives. If this chakra is too weak, we may have trouble feeling connected to our partner or to our work. If this chakra is overactive, we may have a tendency to give too much, or a tendency to feel depressed and a hard time feeling joy. In the case of severe depression, please get in touch with an appropriate medical practitioner.

Properties of a Balanced 2nd Chakra
- Fulfillment in work
- Balanced giving and receiving
- Balanced relationships
- Appreciation for beauty
- Effortless creativity

If this chakra needs adjusting, there are steps that we can take to help balance this area of our lives. To open the chakra you may find it helpful to use the mudra (hand postures) associated with the strengthening of this chakra area.

Keep your hands in your lap, left hand under right hand palms up, and thumbs touching. As you sit, remember to pull your belly button towards your spine. This helps to circulate the energy in the Sacral chakra area, and helps to open the area and make the lower back more flexible. You can do this in a meeting or on the bus, but if you are able to go into a meditative state, all the better. Use the mantra 'VAM' (Sanscrit for compassion and wisdom) to further enhance the experience.

In a Tarot reading, there are a number of cards that are associated with this chakra because they are associated with the creative process. If any of these cards come up, look for the meaning that you associate with that card. Concentrate on the meaning and the image, and always use your own images as well. Meditate on how you can use the information and apply it to yourself.

SACRAL CHAKRA ASSOCIATED TAROT CARDS & KEYWORDS

PRIESTESS: VIRGIN, BEGINNINGS
MOON: FLOW AND CHANGE
SUN: GROWTH AND CREATIVITY
KING OF SWORDS: HIGH IDEALS
SEVEN OF SWORDS: CUNNING, DETERMINATION
KNIGHT OF WANDS: CREATIVE ALCHEMY
SEVEN OF WANDS: ADVERSITY
EIGHT OF CUPS: SHARING
TWO OF CUPS: JOINING
SIX OF DISKS: STRIKING WHILE THE IRON IS HOT
THREE OF DISKS: WORK, ENERGY FLOW

Red - Root or Base chakra
Muladhara

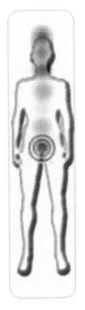

The Base chakra is called Muladhara, which means "root" or "foundation" in Sanskrit. The Root chakra is located around the tailbone - right at the end of the spinal column. This is where the three main *nadis* or energy channels begin.

The Ida, Pingala and Sushumma combine to govern our central nervous system, and this forms the Kundalini energy conduit. The Kundalini is the coil of energy at the base of the spine known as Shakti or serpent power, and with practice, you can learn to release or raise the energy.

Chakra work is designed to help us reach our full potential or "God consciousness." Through yoga, meditation, and other similar disciplines, Kundalini awakens to merge with her husband Shiva in the crown center. "Kundalini is sometimes described as the individual bodily representation of the great cosmic power which creates and sustains the universe. Because each human being is a microcosm of that macrocosm, that power also sustains us."[37]

Tribal instincts form here. Whom we're most comfortable with, our connections to our surroundings, and our grounding or stability, start with this chakra.

Safety and fear of being hurt both psychologically and physically start in this region. Physically, this chakra governs our sense of smell, our large intestine and ability to process elimination, our bones and our adrenal glands (our fight or flight response) all derive from this chakra.

When this chakra is out of balance, you may find you are edgy around people or have trouble letting go of situations. If your Base chakra is weak you may act flighty, or indecisively.

If it is overactive you may be too stodgy, and you may find that physical reality is boring. If you're tired, suffer lower backaches, bloating or feel like you're carrying a heavy load, it could be time for a chakra adjustment.

Properties of a Balanced 1st Chakra
- Feeling safe in the body
- Acute animal instincts
- Good appetite
- Physical prowess

To harmonize this area, we need to listen to the beat of our heart, calm ourselves and allow our consciousness to affect the world. We belong where we are because we have something to learn from where we are. Try not to let painful events overwhelm you; rather, remember that there is a cycle to all things. The passage of time will allow new growth and change to take place – concentrate on grounding where you are. Foster the health of your Base chakra with a hearty meal. Pasta with tomatoes and red wine will help ground you. Share it with friends to help foster belonging, and learn to relax. You do belong, and belonging brings grounding.

Red is the longest wavelength of light that we can perceive. It is reputedly one of the first colors we see when we open our eyes as babies, and it is also one of the colors that can be restored to the color blind with laser surgery. The color red is a complex symbol of blood, birth, anger, passion, life and death in human psychology. In a vast array of Neolithic graves from various countries, red ocher has been found at many sites. Either stored in pots, or dusted over the deceased, it is an emblem of passing and a life of belonging. Red ocher or iron oxide was one of the first paints used by humanity.

A number of Tarot cards are associated with the Root chakra. These cards are associated with grounding, tribal connection, health and security. If any of these cards come up in a Tarot reading, look for ways to integrate the message into your daily activities.

BASE CHAKRA ASSOCIATED TAROT CARDS & KEYWORDS

EMPRESS MOTHER: PRIMORDIAL
STRENGTH CONNECTION: MANIFESTATION
DEVIL - OBSESSION DISRESPECT: ATTACHMENT
TEN OF SWORDS: DISASTER
FIVE OF SWORDS: DISILLUSION, DEFEAT, SHAME
KING OF WANDS: PASSION
TEN OF WANDS: FINALE
KNIGHT OF CUPS: EXPANDING
ACE OF CUPS: PROMISE
SEVEN OF DISKS: LIMIT, RESTRAINT
FOUR OF DISKS: RECHARGE

THE SEVEN MAJOR CHAKRAS

ENDNOTES

1 [p. 11] Stein, Diane. Essential Reiki: A Complete Guide to an Ancient Healing Art. Crossing Press, Ithica, NY. 1995.

2 [p. 12] Lucas, George, Leigh Brackett, Lawrence Kasdan. Star Wars: Episode V - The Empire Strikes Back. Lucasfilm. 1980.

3 [p. 12] Baba, Meher. Coined the term "Over-Soul." Also Essays: First Series on the duality of man's nature by Ralph Waldo Emerson, 1841.
<http://en.wikipedia.org/wiki/Over-soul>
[Accessed: June 12, 2008].

4 [p. 12] Brahman & Atman. Wikipedia Encyclopedia Online.
<http://en.wikipedia.org/wiki/Upanishads>
[Accessed June 12, 2008].

5 [p. 12] Upanishad. Hindu Scriptures. Wikipedia Encyclopedia Online.
< http://en.wikipedia.org/wiki/Upanishad>
[Accessed: June 12, 2008].

6 [p. 12] Buddhism. Wikipedia Encyclopedia Online.
< http://en.wikipedia.org/wiki/Buddhist#The_Four_Noble_Truths>
[Accessed June 15, 2008].

7 [p. 13] Ibid.

8 [p. 13] Huson, Paul. The Devil's Picturebook: The Compleat Guide to Tarot Cards: Their Origins and Their Usage. G. P. Putnam's Sons, New York, NY. 1971.

9 [p. 14] Etheric. The auraic layer in the human energy field in contact with the body. Wikipedia Encyclopedia Online. < http://en.wikipedia.org/wiki/Etheric_body> [Accessed June 12, 2008].

10 [p. 18] Weisstub, EB. "Self as the Feminine Principle." Journal of Analytical Psychology, Jul;42(3):425-52; 1997. <http://www.ncbi.nlm.nih.gov/pubmed/9246929?dopt=Abstract%20Anal%20Psychol%201997%20Oct> [Accessed August 28, 2007].

11 [p. 19] Card, Charles R. "The Emergence of Archetypes in Present-Day Science and Its Significance for a Contemporary Philosophy of Nature." Dynamical Psychology. Victoria: Univ. of Victoria, BC, Canada, 1996. <http://www.compilerpress.atfreeweb.com/Anno%20Card%20Archetypes%20&%20Modern%20Science%201996.htm#The%20Development%20of%20the%20Concept%20of%20Archetype> [Accessed August 28, 2007].

12 [p. 20] Jung, C.G. Collected Works, vol. 6-10 "On the Nature of the Psyche," CW 8, par. 414.

13 [p. 58] Sacrifice."The Sun" Encyclopedia Symbols from Symbols Online. <http://www.symbols.com/encyclopedia/15/151.html> [Accessed March 12, 2007].

14 [p. 67] Steidle, Brian,Gretchen Steidle Wallace. The Devil Came on Horseback: Bearing Witness to the Genocide in Darfur. Public Affairs,New York, NY. 2007. [See page 67]

15 [p. 76] Monaghan, Patricia. O Mother Sun!: A New View of the Cosmic Feminine. Crossing Press, Ithica, NY. 1994.

16 [p. 76] From Mythinglinks.org Weaving Art and Lore. < http://www.mythinglinks.org/ct~weaving.html > [Accessed: June, 21,2007].

17 [p. 78] Vitamin D, Paraphrased from various sources on Web MD.
<http://www.webmd.com >

18 [p. 79] "Ephiphany." Encarta Dictionary.
<http://encarta.msn.com/dictionary_1861608848/epiphany.h tml >

19 [p. 94] Toyoda, Toshiaki. Blue Spring. Omega Micott Inc., Japan. 2001.

20 [p. 95] Golding, William. Lord of the Flies. Penguin, Putnam Group. New
York, NY. 1954.

21 [p. 101] Hesse,Hermann. Siddhartha. Trans. Hilda Rosner (Allegorical
Buddha) Bantam Books,1922, 1951 (U.S.)

22 [p. 102] Ibid.

23 [p. 116] Jennis,Lucas. The Book of Lambspring. English Trans. Adam
McLean. Musaeum Hermeticum. Frankfurt, Germany. 1625.
<http://www.levity.com/alchemy/lambtext.html>
[Accessed: June, 15,2008].

24 [p. 109] Campbell, Joseph, Bill Moyers, Betty Sue Flowers. The Power of
Myth. Doubleday, New York, NY. 1988.

25 [p. 139] "Virtue". Wikipedia Encyclopedia Online.
http://en.wikipedia.org/wiki/Virtue
[Accessed: 6/5/2008].

26 [p. 157] Emoto, Masaru. The Hidden Messages in Water. Trans. David A.
Thayne. Beyond Words Inc., Hillsboro, OR. 2001.

27 [p. 173] "Law of Attraction." Wikipedia Encyclopedia Online.
< http://en.wikipedia.org/wiki/Law_of_Attraction>
[Accessed: 6/16/08].

28 [p. 178] Van Wijka, Roeland, Masaki Kobayashi, Eduard P.A. Van Wijk. "Anatomic characterization of human ultra-weak photon emission with a moveable photomultiplier and CCD imaging" Journal of Photochemistry and Photobiology B: Biology, Volume 83, Issue 1, 3 April 2006, pages 69-76.

29 [p. 188] Nepoleon and the bee symbol.
< http://www.loc.gov/shop/index.php?action=cCatalog.showItem&cid= 6&scid=64&iid=3142 >
[Accessed: 9/19/2007].

30 [p. 193] Watts, Alan W. The Wisdom of Insecurity. Pantheon Books, New York, NY. 1951.

31 [p. 197] Hermes and Io
< http://www.pantheon.org/articles/h/hermes.html >
[Accessed: 7/7/2007]

32 [p. 207] Wills, Pauline. Chakra Workbook: Rebalance Your Body's Vital Energies. Eddison Sadd, London. 2002.

33 [p. 208] Osborn, Gary. "The Gate of God Part 1" From The Book of THoTH Paranormal Research and Discussion Online.
<http://www.book-of-thoth.com/article1542.html>
[Accessed: 9/19/2007].

34 [p. 212] 5th Chakra. "Kundalini Yoga and Chakra Balancing"
< http://www.kundaliniyogablog.com/-2006-09-15-vishuddha-5th-chakra-communication-center/ >
[Accessed: 9/19/2007].

35 [p. 213] Wills, Pauline. Chakra Workbook: Rebalance Your Body's Vital Energies. Eddison Sadd, London. 2002.

36 [p. 216] Ibid.

37 [p. 220] Ibid.

Made in the USA